155 BUSINESS WORDS YOU NEED TO KNOW NOW ★ LELA BARKER

Lucky Break
CONSULTING

155 WORDS YOU NEED TO KNOW:
PRACTICAL WISDOM FOR CREATIVE ENTREPRENEURS

by Lela Barker

www.LuckyBreakConsulting.com

155 Words You Need To Know: Practical
Wisdom for Creative Entrepreneurs
By Lela Barker

Copyright © 2012 by Lela Barker
Cover and Text Design by Jessika Hepburn
Editing by Bethany Learn
Cover Photography by Lisa Rodgers

ISBN: 978-0615737454 (Triple C Press)

Published by:

Triple C Press™
7821 St. Andrews Road #3467
Columbia, SC 29063

Reviews

"Lela where have you been all my life? The guide is out of this ball park + galaxy. Never again will I need to hunt for my dusty Webster dictionary for answers or be too scared of where Google might take me. Your guide is just perfect for go-getters + superhero's on a mission. LOVE IT!"

Mayi Carles: Artist + Creative Coach (Life is Messy Bootcamp)

"Do you know what CPQ is? How about FOB or GMP? Economies of scale? Yep, me neither, until I got my hands on this glossary of goodness. This is one dictionary that will keep you awake from cover to cover! Informative, funny and flat out brilliant, Lela has crafted a resource that is every entrepreneur's best friend. Arming yourself with this complete vocabulary of business terms and definitions will empower you to go into that high profile business meeting or cold call a huge distributor without needing an MBA. Buy it, read it, then take over the world!"

**Jessika Hepburn: Editor+ Community Builder
(Oh My! Handmade)**

"Behold! A complete alphabet of creative entrepreneurship, from "Advertisements" to "Zebras." Actually, there is only one zebra in this book (not plural, sadly.) But you should own it, anyway."

**Alex Franzen: Writer + Teacher + Creative Minx
(AlexandraFranzen.com)**

"New to business? This book from Lela should be your number one go-to resource."

**Erin Giles: Writer + World Changer + Philanthropy Coach
(Rocket Your Revolution)**

*"Lela Barker's book **155 Words You Need to Know: Practical Wisdom for Creative Entrepreneurs** is the dream lucky break every business owner craves. This book is filled with nuggets of insight that only someone who has climbed her way from*

hard times to success could ever teach. With Lela's business, Lucky Break Consulting and this book you will find Lela on the ladder of success right ahead of you with her hand extended backwards offering to help lift you up. You could learn it all the hard way, like Lela did, but the best business move you could make is to glean from Lela's hard earned lessons and take the easier road instead. Forget taking hours of business classes, learn from someone who has been there, done that and paved the road of success with breadcrumbs that are simple enough to digest for anyone to follow."

Kayla Fioravanti: Author
(KaylaFioravanti.com)

*"Lela Barker has condensed her years in the small business school of hard knocks into a resource no entrepreneur should be without. Not only is **155 Words You Need to Know: Practical Wisdom for Creative Entrepreneurs** a user-friendly guide to terms every entrepreneur must understand, but it's also sprinkled with humor and true stories that drive home the specific ideas and mindsets you need to be successful in your business. Like me, you will want to keep this book handy to quickly create context and action steps around every business challenge you face. I highly recommend **155 Words You Need to Know: Practical Wisdom for Creative Entrepreneurs** to everyone who refuses to take, "No" for an answer, and who will stop at nothing to make their entrepreneurial dreams come true."*

Donna Maria Coles Johnson: Founder & CEO
(INDIE Business Network)

*"Fun, creative and down-right awesome, **155 Words You Need to Know: Practical Wisdom for Creative Entrepreneurs** will be your guide helping you go from the small time to the big league. Complicated business terms in a language you understand including creative examples that help you wrap your brain around the concepts. Arm yourself with the knowledge you need to grow your empire and buy your copy now. You can thank me later."*

Isa Maria Seminega: Founder
(Noisette Academy)

I HELP ENTREPRENEURS GET LUCKY...

Dedication

To everyone who has ever dreamed bigger than their current circumstances should dictate, I raise my glass and dedicate this book to you. May you be infused with tenacity, hunger, enthusiasm, and most of all... hope. I'm cheering you on wherever you are.

"What lies behind us and what lies before us are tiny matters compared to what lies within us."

Ralph Waldo Emerson

Acknowledgements

They say it takes a village... and that's true. I've been building my village for many years, and I'd like to take this opportunity to recognize a few of its most cherished citizens who have been in the trenches with me all the while.

Thank you, first and foremost, to my husband Christopher who dances in the shadows but is the very core of my support system. Your willingness to assist in geography homework, to clear a sink full of dishes, to drive children to gymnastics studios and horse stables has provided me the opportunity and flexibility to create a life I truly love. Thank you for occasionally letting me cry it out without the dread of judgment. Thank you for containing your fears and withholding your looks of disapproval upon the announcement that I'm off to another far-flung country. One day I promise to be still. I will likely be 90 and hunched in half by then, but I promise I will eventually be still.

To my children, Chloe and Celie, thank you for renewing my hope each day. Collectively, you embody the genesis of my desire to succeed. I hope that my adventures will inspire you to dream big, stare down your fears, push the envelope and hope for the impossible. Your spunk and compassion inspires me daily to be a better mom and a more engaged inhabitant of the earth. Now, for the love of God... please clean your rooms.

To my parents, whose confidence in my abilities and talents has never wavered, even in moments when I have temporarily lost confidence in myself, thank you for your perpetual cheerleading, your generosity and your chocolate pie. Thank you for always believing that I could be something greater than broke, single and living in your spare bedroom.

To my sister Mimi, whose cancer scare was the catalyst for that first batch of lotion, thank you for the inspiration. Despite our fiercely competitive natures, there is no one else beside whom I'd want to lay in a labor and delivery bed. No one's postpartum legs I will so willingly shave, and no one's children I will ever take such delight in corrupting.

To my baby brother Johnathan, who managed to score an entrepreneurial degree light years ahead of his entrepreneurial sister, I'm immensely excited to have a front-row seat as you define and blaze your own trail. And I forgive you for not taking the job at Bella Luccè®. Though I secretly hope you're still kicking your own ass, but just a little bit...

To Sara, my best friend of 14 years, thank you for being my eternal sounding board and for talking me off the cliffs. I promise to keep you knee-deep in Cranberry Yuzu Sugar Scrub for the rest of your natural days.

To my team at Bella Luccè®, thank you for sharing in this journey. Your dedication and support are the pillars of that company's success and I am ever grateful for the opportunity to work with each of you.

A special nod to my designer Jessika who refused to be intimidated by my ridiculous deadlines. Thank you for putting on another pot of coffee and getting down to business. You're my long lost soul sister, and I look forward to drinking you under the table when I finally make it to Nova Scotia.

And finally, I am particularly grateful for all of the people and situations that presented as obstacles or challenges along the way. From employees gone stark raving mad to accounts gone bankrupt and everything in between, I raise my glass to each of you. The old saying is true: that which doesn't kill us makes us stronger. I'm thrilled to still be kicking, and I appreciate the trials and tribulations. I savor each lesson learned and wish all of you well.

TABLE OF CONTENTS

Introduction

If we had met a decade ago, and you asked me to sum myself up in a few words, these would have been the most likely candidates: broke, broken and desperate. Not a very rosy picture, eh? In 2002, I scooped up my two toddlers and walked away from a hopeless marriage without a dime to my name. I moved across the state to regroup and take refuge at my parent's home, deriving comfort in late night chats with my mom over her famous chocolate pie. But after a few months of solace, I acknowledged that it was time to wind down the pity party and start pulling a plan together. My goal? Find a job that provided both urgently needed income and the flexibility to nurture my sweet girls in the midst of a tsunami of change.

Five years earlier, I had walked away from a full university scholarship at 21 years old after learning that I was simultaneously pregnant and battling cancer -neither of which had been in my master plan. Suddenly, at the ripe old age of 26, I was tasked with creating a life for my two little girls. I had precious few marketable skills, no college degree and zero connections in a new town that was a seven hour drive from all the relationships and support I'd cultivated over the last twenty years. The day that the local steakhouse politely declined my application to be a waitress, I drove endless backroads, doing the "not pretty cry" (you know... *that* one) and contemplating how on earth I would manage to get my life back on track.

It was my mother who first suggested that I take the bath salts and colorful soaps I'd been making as a hobby for the last few years and try to sell them while I looked for a "real" job, of course. I would give them a name, sketch out pricing and start turning up at art festivals and farmer's markets. We reasoned that I could make the products after I tucked the wee ones in for the night, and my mother could watch them on weekends as I peddled my wares.

The next few months proved to be a frenetic whirlwind of research and activity. Just as I was poised to make my humble debut at the Lenoir City Arts Festival, a dear friend made an unexpected offer: She wanted to approach a local boutique with my soaps and lotions in exchange for a 15% cut of any sale. Thinking her mad, I laughed off the idea that any legitimate store would buy products that I had created in a two-quart pot on the stove of my tiny kitchen. But she enjoyed the last laugh when she rang me a few days later to ask how she should address a three thousand dollar check!

Fast forward ten years: Bella Luccè® products have found a home in more than 1,000 spas, salons and boutiques worldwide from Los Angeles to Dubai. They've enjoyed a sellout run on Shop at Home® television and have been featured in the national and international press, from *Southern Living to Life & Style Magazine*. I've collected more than twenty passport stamps as I travel the world on behalf of my company, and I'm home most afternoons by 3:00pm to walk the dogs and greet the girls, now teenagers... where did the time go?

I still don't have that college degree. I've never had a single bank loan, nor a grant, nor a press agent, nor a team of sales reps. My friend Rachel moved to Iowa the next year, bringing her short tenure to a close. Despite all the odds and in the midst of a harsh recession, my company has succeeded beyond my wildest dreams. It's never been easy, and it hasn't always been pretty, but I've been digging my heels into those entrepreneurial trenches for a solid decade. I'm keenly aware of how lonesome and bewildering the entrepreneurial path can be. That's the very genesis of the book you now hold in your hot little hands.

155 Words You Need to Know: Practical Wisdom for Creative Entrepreneurs is the culmination of all the times I wish I'd had a mentor by my side. It's the wisdom that sprung from the countless times someone asked a question during a meeting or presentation using a term I'd never before heard. I would furiously scribble those foreign words down on paper and spend my evenings doing Google® searches to give them context and meaning. This wisdom didn't come from textbooks or sitting through a class; it was hard-won and personally developed through years of trial and error, victories and stumbles, triumphs and tribulations.

The birth of each of my businesses ranks amongst my greatest challenges, but the obstacles I've conquered and the trials I've endured have made the victories taste all the sweeter. While I firmly believe that entrepreneurship is not for the meek or faint of heart, I'm equally convinced that it is a phenomenally empowering, transformative experience. My hope is that the information held within these pages will prove helpful on your journey, that there's a nugget or two buried herein that propels you forward, sparks an idea or encourages you to look at your business with fresh eyes.

Onward and Upward!

Lela Rain Barker
President: Lucky Break Consulting

Order In!

GET READY FOR 155 WORDS YOU NEED TO KNOW

Lucky Break
CONSULTING

ADDITIONAL INSURED: A person or organization that enjoys the benefit of coverage from an insurance policy, in addition to the original purchaser of that policy. For example: Many department stores and retail chains require manufacturers to add them as an "additional insured" to existing liability insurance policies, so that the store can enjoy coverage for damage or injury caused by defective products just as if they were the manufacturer. In doing so, the manufacturer's policy provides primary coverage in case of accident or injury, reducing the loss history for the store, and resulting in lower premiums. Most insurance providers can add additional insureds for a nominal cost.

See also: Liability Insurance.

ADVANTAGES: A marketing term related to, but distinct from, features and benefits. In a nutshell, products and services all have features, which describe something technical about the offering. Those features give the product specific advantages. Those advantages offer the consumer specific benefits, which are what compels them to click the "buy" button or scoop your product off the shelf. If your face cream contains argan oil, that's a feature.

The advantage of that product might be that the cream helps slow transepidermal water loss thanks to the protection provided by the argan oil. Knowing your features from your benefits, and knowing your advantages from your features, helps build marketing campaigns that resonate with consumers and drive sales. It's the difference between *"that product looks lovely"'* and *"Holy cannolis! I need that product in my life."*

See also: Features, Benefits.

ADVERTISEMENT: A form of paid marketing communication designed to persuade an audience to action. Examples might include: a banner ad on a website advertising your services; a coupon in the paper to encourage people to purchase your products; a flyer in neighborhood mailboxes letting locals know of an upcoming event; a half-page ad in a national magazine announcing a new product launch. Well executed advertisements raise awareness, reinforce your brand and call consumers to action.

See also: Advertorial, Editorial, Call to Action.

ADVERTORIAL: An advertisement in a newspaper or magazine designed to mimic editorial coverage rather than paid coverage. Advertorials are a sneaky little trick, as their content would lead readers to believe that the magazine is raving on Susie's Snickerdoodle Cookies. In reality, Susie forked over a check to the publishing company. Advertorials have risen in popularity as advertisers have come to the realization that editorial coverage more effectively influences readers when compared to traditional advertising. Advertorials represent an advertiser's way of having their cake and eating it, too. If the words "this is an advertisement" appear in print anywhere on the page, consider that confirmation of an advertorial.

See also: Editorial, Advertisement.

ART SPECIFICATIONS: The guidelines issued by a particular printer detailing the manner in which graphic art files need to be prepared for commercial printing. Art specifications typically identify the file type, resolution, bleed, and color process in addition to whether or not fonts need to be converted to outlines. To save time, money and sanity: you should always inquire about the art specifications of a particular printing company before placing an order. Doing so will ensure that graphic files will be prepared according to their specifications the first time around.

Also, it's important to know the Golden Rule of printing: always, always, always ask for a proof and comb through it with laser-like scrutiny.

See also: Dots Per Inch (DPI), Ready Graphics.

BALANCE: The elusive yin and yang craved by entrepreneurs who own a business but don't want to be wholly consumed by it. Balance means finding a way to stare down your daily "to do" list without losing your sanity and enjoying the ability to dream about something other than your company every night. It's a vital element of any burgeoning empire. Entrepreneurship often requires work weeks that would curl the toes of the 40-hour set. It means working on some weekends and often working late because the responsibility ultimately rests on your shoulders. However, burnout is a very real and tangible beast and burning yourself to a crisp doesn't ultimately propel your business forward, and it can compromise your health and relationships. Implementing practical efficiencies and strategies is critical to long-term success.

BATCH NUMBER: The unique number assigned to a batch of product (typically personal care products or food) by its manufacturer to track ingredients, production technique and date of manufacture. The batch number is ultimately tied to a batch record, which further traces the quantity and origin of the raw materials, the parties involved in its creation, the procedures that brought it to life, and the results of any testing conducted before its release for sale. Even if a company aspires to keep all of those lovely, detailed records, if they're not tied to a specific batch number, then it's impossible to close the loop of traceability.

See also: *Batch Record, Good Manufacturing Practices, Lot Number, Microbiology Testing, Standard Operating Procedure.*

BATCH RECORD: A permanent report detailing the specifics of a particular batch of perishable products, be that a batch of eye shadow, bath salts, pumpkin muffins, chocolate truffles, or mango tea. Batch records are a critical component of any quality control program.

If it's impossible to determine how something was made, is there any certainty that it was made properly? With the right ingredients? According to an agreed recipe or formula? At the right temperature? How can a consumer determine when it expires? They can't, and if you sell perishable goods without those certainties, you expose your company to a world of worry and liability: Were those pumpkin muffins baked properly to ensure customers don't develop food poisoning? Could this eye shadow be contaminated with microbes that cause an eye infection? *"Why the hell do these truffles taste bad... they can't be that old!"* You get the idea.

Please, for the love of all things holy, standardize your manufacturing procedures, create batch records and assign batch numbers.

See also: *Batch Number, Good Manufacturing Practices, Lot Number, Microbiology Testing, Quality Control Program, Standard Operating Procedure.*

BENEFITS: A strategic marketing concept, benefits are what compel consumers to purchase particular goods or services. They are related to (but distinct from) features and advantages. A benefit describes specifically how your handkerchiefs, stationary, or unicorn horns will make a consumer's life more stylish, more abundant, more convenient, etc.

Let's try a practical example...

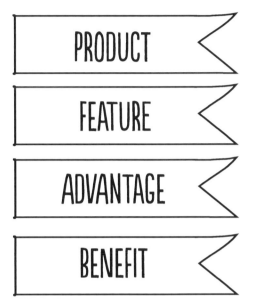

PRODUCT Lela's Sugar -Free Green Apple Pie

FEATURE My pie is made with Stevia®, an all-natural sweetener.

ADVANTAGE Because Stevia® contains virtually no calories, my pie contains half the calories of traditional apple pies made with sugar.

BENEFIT Endure one less hour on the elliptical this week...have your pie and eat it, too!

See also: Features, Advantages.

BLOG: An online journal which enables the author to make entries which are displayed and archived in chronological order. A well-executed business blog engages consumers, builds collaborations, drives sales, and enhances company credibility.

There are many types of blog software available. Much of it is free to the public, boasting a variety of features (Reference Appendix D for links and suggestions). I've been a loud and proud advocate of blogging for almost a decade, but I couldn't possibly count the number of times other small business owners have told me that they shy away from it because they're not sure what to say. Well, my fingers are planted firmly in my ears. I'm of the strong opinion that if you own a business, you need to be blogging. Period.

Take these ideas out for a spin:

IF MY BUSINESS IS A...	...THEN I COULD BLOG ABOUT
Organic Bath & Body Company	Pictures from batches of product while in production; short articles extolling the benefit of a particular ingredient used; testimonials from people who adore my hand cream; a recipe for a DIY lip scrub recipe made with items found in every kitchen pantry; profiles of stores that carry my products; pictures of clients using my products; links to articles announcing new research about the benefits of organic goods; recipes that highlight easy-to-create wholesale meals; tips for living green everyday...
Local Bakery Specializing in Custom Sugar Cookies	Pictures of cookies I make each day; pictures from parties or celebrations where my cookies are featured; shout-outs to clients who are celebrating anniversaries, weddings, graduations and birthdays who are incorporating my cookies into the celebration; recipes for my favorite childhood treats culled from my mother's cookbook; a daily announcement of what baked goods I have in the oven; what coffee I have on to brew; a secret word which- when uttered by the next 5 clients who walk in the door- yields a free cookie with every $20 order...
Letterpress Company	Behind-the-scenes snapshots that illustrate how letterpress items are created; an article detailing the history of letterpress art; links to pieces of vintage letterpress that you personally collect; profiles of

Letterpress Company continued

...your favorite graphic design artists; your latest gig poster, wedding invitation or greeting card; tips for writing short and sweet letters that hold meaning; corporate etiquette tips that, of course, mention the importance of a handwritten thank you, and a link to your thank you card offerings; a design contest where consumers vote on your next letterpress design...

Jewelry Collection

Pictures of customers wearing your jewelry; links to articles about current color trends; outfits that you pull together from various online stores, accented with your jewelry; gemstone profiles which teach clients about the history, characteristics and origins of the stones used in your pieces; snapshots of pieces in progress; exhibits of custom work; tips for accessorizing in a flash; pictures of the jewelry your grandmother passed down to you; places or people that inspire your creations...

Portrait Photography Service

Snapshots from recent photo shoots; pictures from exotic locales where you'd love to shoot; tips for being more relaxed during photo shoots; an article describing how to style makeup and hair for photo shoots; shout-outs to clients who are celebrating special days or accomplishments, featuring a picture from a past photo shoot; information on what kind of high-tech gear you use; links to websites that can create custom greetings cards, t-shirts, coffee mugs and calendars using your photography...

BOOTSTRAPPING: A method used when starting a company in which a significant portion of profits are typically reinvested into the company to fuel growth. Bootstrapping is a beautiful thing because it involves minimal external resources or capital. As banks have slowed their rate of lending, bootstrapping has become more of a reality for entrepreneurs, especially women. I've personally bootstrapped Bella Luccè® (my bath and body company) from a $500 investment in my petite kitchen to a thriving international company, sold in more than a thousand spas worldwide and headquartered out of a 7,500 square-foot facility.

Yes, it really is possible to build a small empire without the benefit of a trust fund, angel investor or bank loan. Some people believe that's almost as probable as a winged fairy collecting teeth from beneath children's pillows and shining them into stars, but the proof is in the pudding. Bootstrapping typically translates into a slower acceleration rate for young companies, but that slower ascension in sales provides benefits of its own:

1. Bootstrapping provides entrepreneurs adequate time to test the marketplace and refine their product offerings and packaging before making large investments.

2. Products which are bootstrapped often get to market faster because they bypass the cycle of raising capital.

3. Bootstrapping entrepreneurs are traditionally more efficient with their spending, because they can't spend what they don't have.

4. A slower rate of growth allows companies to refine procedures and implement efficiencies to get them to scale, thus avoiding the *"Oh hell, how will we make 10,000 of these?"* moments on tight delivery deadlines.

5. Bootstrappers retain ownership and control over their companies, which not only allows them to stay true to their original vision, it can also lead to larger paydays down the road. Suppose you surrender 90% ownership in your company to a venture capitalist while your business is in its infancy in exchange for a $750,000 investment. In five years, your company is raking in revenues of $4 million, but your share of that revenue is just $400,000. Now suppose you exclude outside investment and instead pour $40,000 of your savings into your own business and bootstrap that bad boy all the way to the bank. In five years, your annual revenue totals $1 million. Your share of that revenue? ONE MILLION DOLLARS. *Ca-ching!*

BRAND DILUTION:

If my "counting to ten" skills weren't as strong, I'd swear that the term brand dilution had four letters. It doesn't, but it might as well. Brand dilution is a decision or series of decisions that weaken, rather than empower, the core brand. The causes and catalysts are numerous: poorly conceived collaborations such as working with another designer whose core audience is mainstream Americana when you're designing luxury goods; partnering with another company whose reputation is less than stellar; poorly planned brand extensions and overuse of a brand name.

THE CREATION OF A 1000 FORESTS IS IN ONE ACORN. ★ R.W. EMERSON

Ponder these examples of brand dilution:

"New" Coke®: This poorly planned brand extension was abandoned three months after launch thanks to an intense public backlash.

Virgin®: Richard Branson's empire now has its tentacles in a dizzying array of goods including hotels, airlines, music, mobile service, vodka, casinos, umbilical cord blood banks, and space tourism. Some of those industry expansions have been wildly successful. Others have lagged behind.

Martha Stewart®: She's lent her name to damn near everything: dog leashes, magazines, TV shows, cookie cutters, shower curtains, paint, carpet, bath towels, and craft kits. While the Martha Stewart® brand was once exclusively associated with lifestyle prestige goods, her collaboration with budget retailer Kmart® negatively impacted that once golden reputation. No one need to weep for Martha; she employs 500+ people and heads up an impressive empire, but the prevailing consensus is that the brand itself doesn't have the "blue blood" exclusivity it once commanded.

Just as the scorching sun can ruin a tall glass of sweet iced tea in the Deep South by quickly melting an abundance of ice cubes, so too can a power-brand be ruined by dilution.

You have the power to stop brand dilution in its tracks by:

- Strategically cultivating your collaborative network by designing collaborations whose participants share commonality amongst your primary customer
- Safeguarding collaborations by ensuring that the company you're climbing into bed with possess a strong, healthy brand reputation
- Ensuring that new product launches expand market share rather than cannibalize your current market share
- Limiting growth and protecting your brand's core

The double nemesis of brand dilution? Focus and vigilance.

See also: *Branding, Ideal Client.*

BRANDING: The process of creating a unique image for products and services.
Sounds simple right? Wrong! *insert buzzer sound* Branding is a complex creature. It's the sum total of a number of parts: logo, packaging, website design, business cards, social media interaction, website copy, brochures, and catalog. It's your story, pitch, product photography, head shot, packing slips, email signature. Yes, even pricing. And on and on. The signs of a tight brand? Harmony among those elements and consistent messaging across all of those elements.

Do this for me: grab one of everything- every piece of paper or packaging related to your venture that a client might see. Spread it all across your living room floor. Grab the laptop, open it up and punch up your website. Now sit in the midst of it all, laptop in hand, website at the ready. Take a long hard look... What is your brand saying to the public? Is it consistent? Is it clear? Is it strong? If you're not satisfied, identify your weaknesses and work towards cohesion.

See also: *Brand Dilution, Business Card, Logo, Niche, Pitch, Packaging, Pricing Strategy, Trade Dress, Trademark.*

BUSINESS CARD: A pocket-sized bit of brilliant marketing, business cards contain key contact information for a company or individual. Well-designed business cards serve as an introduction to the brand and invite further contact. Every business card should display the company name, personal name, title, phone number, email, and website. It's not uncommon to see social media accounts included as well. Say it with me: *Never leave home without a few of your business cards tucked inside your wallet, briefcase or portfolio.* Never, ever. Never. Ever.

See also: Branding, Networking.

BUSINESS LICENSE: A permit (typically issued by the county, city or state) that formally recognizes the right to operate a business. Unless your company headquarters is located on the planet Mars, you'll likely need one. The process is often fantastically simple, so no need to be intimidated. The one-two punch of starting a new business?

　　1: Define the business structure.
　　2: Get a business license.

Easy peasy. Be prepared to pay a small fee for the license. Yes, that means you're putting the government on notice that you're an official entity. Yes, that means you'll be paying taxes. But wait! Don't you want to be a big girl business? It's hard to build empires without proper permitting, and you *are* all about building an empire, aren't you?

See also: Business Structure.

BUSINESS PLAN: The master plan for world domination. Or at a minimum: the selected strategy for the next few years. Business plans don't have to be formal or fancy, but they do need to be done. These blueprints summarize financial and operational objectives for a period of years (1, 3, 5, etc.). It's a living document, which means it can and should evolve as the company grows. Listen closely: You are not a nomad, my friend. You are not meant to wander aimlessly in the desert. Have a plan and sketch it out.

Business plans for internal use (those that are created exclusively for planning purposes) can take virtually any form.

- Start by defining current and future opportunities.

- Next up: present challenges.

- Now, make a strategic plan for capitalizing on those opportunities and minimizing those challenges.

Business plans designed for external audiences are a little hairier, as they're typically prepared for the eyes of lenders and investors and include a myriad of financial details: cash flow statements, pro-forma balance sheets, income statements, etc. If you're not chasing funding, skip the external business plan. At a minimum, though, whip out your internal business plan and breathe new life into it each January.

BUSINESS STRUCTURE: The organizational framework which directs a company's commercial activities. Every company operating within the United States is legally obligated to put the government on notice with regard to what type of business structure they're using. The three most common structures for small business are: sole proprietorships, partnerships and limited liability corporations. Each structure has specific reporting and licensing requirements and each has distinct advantages and disadvantages. Most companies begin as sole proprietorships and then change their official structure over time as the business evolves. But whatever you do, choose a business structure and get legal ASAP.

See also: *Business License.*

BUYER: A person whose job it is to scout, screen and select merchandise for purchase on behalf of a large organization or company. Making life easy for the buyer gives your product a leg up on the competition, hastens purchasing and increases the likelihood of reorders. To woo buyers, companies should:

- Offer clear and reasonable wholesale terms
- Provide innovative products at attractive prices
- Institute solid merchandising principles
- Bring stellar customer service to each and every sale
- Generate media buzz for their products

See also: *Open To Buy, Stockist.*

CALL TO ACTION: A message which urges and influences the audience to take action. Calls to action are critical components of any successful marketing campaign and may be incorporated into webpages, television commercials and/or print advertisements, to name a few. Examples include "call now" or "click here." You've energized your audience; now tell them what to do next! A marketing campaign without a call to action is like a day without sunshine. A birthday cake without candles. A bowl of pasta without a sprinkling of Parmesan. You get the idea...

See also: Advertisement.

DILIGENCE IS THE MOTHER OF GOOD FORTUNE. ★ BENJAMIN DISRAELI

CASE PACK QUANTITY (CPQ): The number of like items (single SKU) that must be purchased at a given time. Case pack quantities are determined by the manufacturer or distributor. Multiple factors can influence CPQ, among them:

- If the product is made fresh, how many units are created from a batch?

- If components of a finished product must be ordered, then the CPQ may be determined by the minimum number of components the manufacturer must purchase to complete the project.

- If the items will be shipped, then how will the items be packaged for transit? How many fit in a box?

- If the manufacturer envisions a robust retail display of their offerings, then how many look good on a store shelf?

Pricing for wholesale accounts is often described both in terms of price per case and price per unit.

See also: Stock Keeping Unit (SKU), Wholesale Terms.

CASH FLOW: In its simplest form, cash flow is the movement of money into or out of a business. Negative cash flow means that the business is spending more than it takes in over a given time. Positive cash flow is a surplus; receiving more money in a given period of time than is spent.

All businesses of every size must ensure they have adequate cash flow to pay their bills, keep the lights on and keep the staff running. It's one thing to land a super-impressive distribution deal and a rather different experience to land that deal on a Net 90 payment plan and then struggle to keep the doors open while you wait for that beloved check. That whole *"I'll gladly pay you Tuesday for a hamburger today"* shtick? That only works with *Popeye®*, not with landlords and the IRS.

See also: Net Terms.

CATALOG: A comprehensive guide to your products and company, generated in a digital or print format. A smart catalog should feature contact information at the top or bottom of every page, full-color photos of each product, descriptions and dimensions of each product and available variants: color, scent, size, etc.). In addition, catalogs should include a compelling cover, some biographical information about the company and various calls to action. If you sprinkle client testimonials or prominent press hits into the mix, all the better.

There are a few ways to tackle pricing. Some companies print prices right in the catalog, while others slip a price sheet into the catalog which is a viable option if you anticipate potential price increases before the next catalog goes to print. Still others ask you to contact the company for pricing. That last option is my least favorite because the number of potential buyers lost in the purchasing process is directly proportional to the number of hoops you ask them to jump through before closing the sale.

See also: Line Sheet, Sell Sheet.

CAUSE MARKETING: Collaborative marketing campaigns which combine the efforts of a for-profit entity with a non-profit organization for the mutual benefit of each. Well executed campaigns attract new customers, increase brand loyalty, boost brand credibility and attract media attention. Cause marketing can take various shapes.

Let's peek at a few...

COMPANY	DONATION	TYPE
Becca's Baby Booties	Donates 1 hand knit blanket for every 20 pairs of hand knit baby booties sold	Donation of X items for every Y items sold
Martha's Munchtastic Muffins	Donates muffins which are close to their expiration date to a local homeless shelter	Donations of valuable product the company would otherwise be scrapping
Sophie's Scrumptious Scrubs	Donates 5% of the retail price of every body scrub sold to a youth mentoring program	A percentage of overall revenue or revenue from a particular product is donated in cash
Greta's Gorgeous Graphics	Donates 5 hours of graphic design work each month to the school Greta's daughter attends	Donation of in-kind services

One caveat: Your nonprofit beneficiary should never learn of the collaboration from your website, blog, social media acticity or press release. Reach out in advance and begin building a relationship.

See also: Corporate Philanthropy.

CEASE & DESIST (C&D):
Communications sent from an aggrieved party to an offender, demanding that the offender stop activity which the aggrieved party deems to be a violation of their rights. Let's assume that an established company starts marketing a similar product under a name for which your company has secured a federally registered trademark. Your first step (after taking a long walk somewhere pretty, pouring yourself a glass of wine and taking a few slow, deep breaths) will likely be to send the other party a formal request that they discontinue the action you believe to be a violation.

Cease and Desist letters should identify perceived violations, cite specific law, detail expected corrective measures and define a timeline for action. Since they can be prepared by an individual or an attorney, many small businesses compose the first "shot across the bow" themselves and then defer to a licensed attorney if the offender fails to take the requested corrective measures. Cease and Desist Orders differ from letters in that they are issued officially by a court of law in response to an action filed by an aggrieved party.

See also: *Copyright, Infringement, Intellectual Property, Registered Mark, Trade Dress, Trademark.*

CHALLENGE TESTING: The clinical test, conducted by a qualified laboratory, to ensure the long-term efficacy of preservative systems in cosmetic formulations. The test is performed by repeatedly introducing common microbes into a product sample to determine if the preservation system in place is capable of prohibiting microbial growth. The FDA recommends that all products be challenge tested before distribution.

CHARGEBACK: The forcible withdrawal of funds from a merchant's bank account, initiated when a cardholder disputes a transaction. Chargebacks can be requested by consumers if goods or services are not delivered as promised or in instances where the amount charged is in excess of the amount owed. On such occasions, consumers may contact their credit card company to file an official complaint about the transaction. Banks will automatically draft the payment from the merchant's account and send notification of the chargeback, with a specific deadline for response.

Merchants traditionally have less than ten days to submit proof of delivery and proof of purchase in order to invalidate the chargeback and reclaim the funds. Unfortunately, identity theft is a frequent problem for businesses of all sizes and cardholders who have had their credit card information stolen may need to file a chargeback against a merchant that fulfilled the order as placed, resulting in a net loss for the business. Unscrupulous customers sometimes take advantage of consumer protection laws and attempt to file a chargeback in an otherwise legitimate transaction.

The good news is that merchants can take action to reduce the probability of chargebacks by:

- Clearly stating refund and return policies at the point of sale
- Ensuring that transactions are entered into point-of-sale terminals only once
- Confirming that canceled transactions are properly voided

E-commerce merchants processing online orders should capture CVV codes and use address verification on all orders. Finally, keep eyes peeled for unusual activity such as a single customer placing orders in rapid succession or an order total which greatly exceeds your average ticket amount. Beware, small businesses: frequent chargebacks will not only cost your company money, but they may lead to the loss of your ability to accept credit cards as a form of payment. Boo hiss!

See also: *Payment Methods.*

COLD CALL: The process of approaching potential clients, typically stockists, to introduce your product or service in any situation where the potential client was not expecting the interaction. While I freely concede that the words "cold" and "call" contain four letters, I assure you that they need not be "bad" four letter words. Cold calls, when thoroughly researched and appropriately timed, can yield remarkable results.

A few tips to point you in the right direction and assuage your cold-calling fears:

- Carefully research the prospective account and ensure you're a good fit before making your approach.
- Schedule specific appointments rather than saying "I'll pop in sometime on Thursday."
- Grease the wheels by offering affordable promotional items or complimentary product samples whenever possible.
- Ensure that your pitch is focused, confident and succinct.
- Know when to declare "Uncle!" If you've engaged the account several times and made your best effort, but they don't seem interested, then move on and refocus your efforts elsewhere.

COLLABORATION: A supportive arrangement between parties who are working towards a common goal. Collaborations can have many incarnations: between allies in the same industry and between associates in very different industries. They may be long term or short term with a specific goal and limited timeline. Examples could include a soap manufacturer who has just moved into their first commercial facility offering space to a fellow soap artisan for a fee on days of the week when the workspace is otherwise unused. An artist could partner with a small stationary company to launch a series of limited edition greeting cards.

Successful collaborations depend on three things:

1. Wisely choosing collaboration partners who possess a solid reputation
2. Ensuring that the arrangement is a win/win for both parties
3. Clearly defining (with documentation!) the expectations and responsibilities inherent in the partnership

See also: *Networking.*

COLLATERAL MATERIALS: Printed materials used to support and reinforce a marketing campaign. Examples include: brochures, shelf talkers, catalogs, and point-of-purchase displays. Executing effective, visually appealing collateral materials is a fine art. The secret? Cohesive branding elements.

See also: *Catalog, Point of Purchase (POP) Display, Shelf Talker.*

COLLECT ON DELIVERY (COD): A payment method that ensures payment for products upon delivery rather than at the time of order placement. Traditionally, the courier (UPS®, FedEx®, freight truck driver or company delivery person) collects a check, money order or cash to satisfy the full balance of the invoice immediately upon delivery. Merchandise cannot be released by the courier until payment is collected in full. However, if the recipient fails to pony up the funds, the shipment is returned to the sender, who is then expected to pay the shipping fees incurred both ways (i.e. to the original recipient and back again to the shipper). CODs were more prevalent before the advent of electronic payments, but some companies still prefer to operate on those terms.

See also: *Payment Options.*

COMMERCIAL INVOICE: A key document in foreign trade, commercial invoices provide specific details of cargo and the parties involved in a given transaction. They serve as the foundation by which tariffs and taxes are calculated on inbound shipments. Though there is no official format, commercial invoices should contain:

- The company name and complete contact details of both the shipping and receiving parties
- A description of the goods being sold
- The country of manufacture
- The harmonized code for each product within the shipment

Flip to the back of this book and refer to Appendix B to discover a groovy database that identifies harmonized codes for every product in the universe.

See also: *Export Pricing, Harmonized Code, Pro Forma Invoice.*

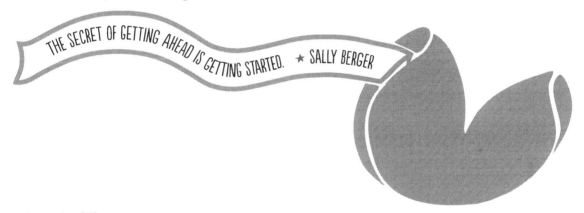

THE SECRET OF GETTING AHEAD IS GETTING STARTED. ★ SALLY BERGER

COMMISSION: A fixed fee or percentage paid to a salesperson or agent for securing or facilitating a commercial sale. The commission is mutually agreed upon by the two parties (the manufacturer and the salesperson or agent) in consideration of their efforts. If businesses plan to utilize sales representatives to increase exposure and secure sales for their widget, they can anticipate some sort of sales commission. I hope your selected pricing strategy accounts for that expense!

See also: *Pricing Strategy, Sales Representative.*

COMPETITION: A term that describes the rivalry between sellers who are striving to achieve the same goals, namely to gain market share and increase their profits. Rare is the modern industry that is devoid of competition. Generally speaking, competitive rivalry is a healthy condition, which encourages all parties in an industry to work leaner and smarter while driving innovation.

However, some small businesses (and solopreneurs in particular) risk becoming consumed by their competition: watching it, imitating it and eliminating it. That's not healthy for them personally, for their companies or for the marketplace. Should entrepreneurs keep an eye on their competition? Certainly. Knowing the features and costs of similar goods is important. Observing trends in marketing strategies is wise. But one shouldn't infringe on a competitor's intellectual property or attempt to unearth their proprietary information. Play fair kids!

See also: *Infringement, Intellectual Property, Proprietary Information.*

CONSIGNMENT: A type of sale in which the possession of goods is transferred, but ownership is retained until a purchase and ensuing payment is made. In the example of a consignment shop: the consignor (the manufacturer of the product) offers the consignee (the seller of the product) the opportunity to make the sale on their behalf. Once the sale is made, the consignor collects payment and forwards it to the consignee, minus a flat fee or percentage of the sale in consideration of their efforts and shelf space. Consignment arrangements can be quite lucrative but crafting a strong consignment contract is paramount. Stores frequently favor consignment arrangements because they present an opportunity to stock shelves with a minimum investment in inventory.

COPYRIGHT: A legal protection enacted by the government which guarantees the rights of an original creator of a specific work. Some examples of original works that qualify for copyright protection include, but are not limited to: literary works of all kinds such as books, webpages, brochures, music, sound recordings, photographs and databases. Copyrights restrict the ability of others to perform, publish, display, or distribute the original work.

For small business owners, copyright works in both directions: you need to ensure that the content you're producing is original and doesn't infringe upon someone else's copyright. Conversely, you also need to ensure that others aren't infringing upon your copyrighted works to make a quick buck. Policing your copyrights and trademarks can be an especially maddening endeavor if not properly managed. Refer to Appendix D for key technologies that can boost monitoring efforts.

See also: Cease & Desist, Infringement, Intellectual Property.

CORPORATE PHILANTHROPY: Resources given by a company to a nonprofit organization. Don't let that fancy "corporate" word fool you... small businesses are often champions of corporate philanthropy.

That altruism can take the form of:

- **Cash Donations:** five percent of the price of every pair of earrings sold or three percent of total sales this year or $1 for every dress pattern sold

- **Services:** a graphic design company donates one logo and branding package to a local nonprofit each year or all employees of a single company volunteer to serve meals in a soup kitchen one day each quarter

- **Goods:** donating 100 bars of handmade soap to the local women's shelter each holiday season or all artisan-baked bread that is a day past its expiration being offered to a local food bank

Giving back not only feels great, it also inspires clients to model the behavior. I strongly recommend that every small businesses identify a passion, match it to a need in the local or international community and build corporate philanthropy into the foundation of the company from the very first day.

The difference between cause marketing and corporate philanthropy? Cause marketing is a type of corporate philanthropy which is publicly announced and integrated into a marketing campaign. Corporate philanthropy may or may not be publicly announced and/or collaboratively incorporated into the overall marketing strategy.

See also: Cause Marketing.

COST OF GOODS SOLD (COGS): In their most basic form, COGS are the combined expenses involved in bringing a product to market.

For manufacturers, those costs include:

- **Raw Materials:** the tangible components that compose your final product plus product packaging
- **Freight Costs:** the fees paid to have all of those raw materials delivered to a location
- **Labor Expenses**: what it costs to pay someone to make that product
- **Overhead Expenses**: workspace rent, utilities, insurance, phone and internet systems, marketing and advertising, etc.

If you don't know your COGS, you don't know your profit. If you don't know your profit, how do you know if you're just keeping busy or actually moving the ball forward? And if you are just staying busy and not moving the ball forward, then why are you in business at all? COGS people. Know 'em. Don't guess, KNOW.

RAW MATERIALS + LABOR + OVERHEAD + FREIGHT = COGS

See also: Labor, Overhead, Raw Materials.

CREDIT APPLICATION: A request for an extension of credit when purchasing goods or services. At a minimum, the written document should indicate the complete contact information of the entity or individual requesting credit, multiple trade references that have previously extended credit to the applicant and a bank reference. Additionally, the credit application should outline the terms under which credit is offered, including interest rates, maximum credit limit and how late payments will be handled. The information contained on the application is then verified before a lending decision is made. As a small business, you'll likely be applying for credit terms with some of your vendors and, as you grow, extending credit terms to some of your clients. Properly managing both varieties is paramount to your company's success and long term viability. Whatever you do, always ensure that credit applications are signed, dated and filed.

See also: Net Terms, Payment Options, Trade Reference.

CROWDFUNDING:
An approach to raising capital for new companies or creative projects which collects small donations from a large number of ordinary people, usually via internet campaigns. Rewards are often promised at certain donation levels, but no repayment or ownership in the company is expected. Many young companies and creative projects are looking to crowdfunding as a source of additional or alternate capital to get their businesses off the ground. Refer to Appendix F for crowdfunding resources.

See also: *Bootstrapping.*

CUSTOMER SERVICE:
The method by which trust and loyalty are created amongst customers. It is composed of (and its success dictated by) every direct interaction with a customer, and includes both company policies and responses to crisis. A customer service foundation is much bigger than a simple return policy. It's how swiftly customer inquiries receive a response, how defective products are handled, how quickly orders are shipped, how deliverables are packaged, etc. This fundamental concept can make or break a business.

My favorite quote on the subject comes from Maya Angelou, who most assuredly was not speaking of customer service when she uttered these words. *"I've learned that people will forget what you said, people will forget what you did, but people will never forget how you made them feel."* That's the very essence of customer service!

See also: *One Time Courtesy, Return Policy, Wholesale Terms.*

CUSTOMS BROKER:
An individual or company who specializes in the minutiae of customs law, import and export regulations, customs classification, trade documentation, and tariff schedules. Brokers act as agents on behalf of the importer or exporter to prepare and submit all documents for clearing goods through customs upon arrival. International transportation arrangements are often mind-numbingly complex, and customs brokers are whizzes at navigating the paperwork and logistics needed to avoid costly delays, fines and even seizure of goods. Brokerage services are an optional but wise investment for small businesses. Their proficiency saves you time and money while also providing an established trade network of connections. If they deal in volume, brokers can often negotiate lower rates for physical transport of goods via air or ocean. They are sometimes known as "freight forwarders."

See also: *International Distribution.*

DISTRIBUTORS: A company that purchases non-competing products and houses them temporarily before reselling them to retailers or end consumers. Retail distribution models go something like this:

MANUFACTURER —› END CONSUMER

Wholesale distribution models look more like this:

MANUFACTURER —› WHOLESALER —› END CONSUMER

But a distribution model adds yet another step to the process:

MANUFACTURER —› DISTRIBUTOR —› WHOLESALER —› END CONSUMER

Keep in mind that everyone in that chain (save for the end consumer) is looking to realize a profit. Distributors can be key allies domestically and, most especially, overseas. They order in large volume and frequently offer technical assistance and after-market support to consumers. The secret to success with a distributor? Choosing partners wisely and ensuring that all COGS have been accurately calculated to protect profit margins.

See also: *Pricing Strategy.*

DOOR: A single retail location. If a potential client requesting wholesale information indicates that they have "four doors," they are specifying that their company operates four separate retail locations. Four is better than one. And twelve is better than four. Hooray for doors!

DOTS PER INCH (DPI): A measurement of printer resolution which indicates how many "dots" there are per inch of graphic. DPI is a type of art specification used by printers. The more dots there are per inch, the finer the detail on a picture and the clearer it will render in the finished product. For example, let's assume you're creating a label for your new line of party dip mixes. If the printer you've selected indicates that they need the finished art files in a "300 DPI" format, they're expressing that the file you hand off to them must have a minimum of 300 dots of ink for every square inch of image in order to yield the highest quality image. Likewise, when the editor at your favorite glossy calls to say they're excited to feature your jewelry collection in an upcoming issue, they'll likely ask for pictures in a specific DPI to ensure that the items look as smashing in print as they do in person.

Bloggers and web developers use the term, too. In digital formats, they reference pixels per inch (PPI) instead of DPI, and this represents a certain color or brightness. You might be familiar with the oft-heard term "high resolution." High resolution images contain more pixels in a given area to yield a cleaner, sharper image. The resolution needed for actual printed items is much higher than it is for digitally yielded images.

When asked for "high resolution" images, it's safe to assume:

- **250-300 dpi** minimum for images which are to be physically printed

- **72-100 dpi** minimum for images that will be displayed on a computer screen

In the same way that your printer may indicate their preferred DPI, so too may the blogger who's featuring your custom-printed greeting cards in an upcoming holiday piece. If you want to land the free press, then you must be able to quickly deliver the images in the format requested. Rest assured: No one is sitting around, tiny pointer and magnifying glass in-hand, individually enumerating the dots. Technology can yield the DPI with the click of a button on graphics programs, so we can save the magical counting elves for more exciting tasks!

See also: Art Specifications, Print Ready Graphics, Product Photography.

E-commerce: Short for "electronic commerce." Any sale made via computer is classified as an e-commerce sale. Though the vast majority of sales in the United States are still made via traditional methods, the growth of the e-commerce segment is outpacing growth in traditional sectors, typically by multiple percentage points. According to a report released by the U.S. Commerce Department in August of 2012, e-commerce sales made between April 1 - June 30, 2012 totaled $54.8 billion (with a b!) dollars and one out of every twenty sales made during the period was made via computer.[1]

What does that mean for you?

- You need a website. Stat.

- You need an e-commerce platform which enables online purchasing.

See also: Search Engine Optimization (SEO).

ECONOMY OF SCALE: A term that refers to the cost advantages companies enjoy when expanding. For example: If a spa orders 10 sugar scrubs from your bath and body company, you'll probably fill that order by purchasing a 5lb. bag of sugar from your local grocery costing $4 (or $.80 per pound). However, if you receive an order for 100 sugar scrubs, you're more likely to purchase that sugar in a 25lb. bag at a restaurant supply company at a cost of $14 (or $.56 per pound), thus saving $.24 per pound of sugar.

In another example, let's assume your company manufacturers wooden furniture for children and you rent a workshop at a cost of $500 per month. If one person working 40 hours a week can produce 10 pieces of furniture each month, then each of those ten pieces of furniture "costs" the company the equivalent of $50 in rent. However, if orders increase enough to justify two workers working 40 hours a week to produce 20 pieces of furniture per month, then the rent expenses associated with a single piece of furniture are reduced by half, to just $25 per piece. Viola! That's the magic of the economy of scale.

See also: *Cost of Goods Sold (COGS), Pricing Strategy, Raw Material.*

LUCK IS WHAT HAPPENS WHEN PREPARATION MEETS OPPORTUNITY ★ SENECA

EDITORIAL: Press coverage in either traditional print or digital media which expresses the opinion of an editor. Editorial coverage differs from advertising in that no money changes hands in consideration of the feature. Examples of editorial coverage might include a *Ten Hot Looks for Fall* piece in a fashion magazine featuring your scarf or perhaps an article entitled *Behold The Power of Pomegranate* which offers a plug to your pomegranate face wash. Editorial coverage is free (ca-ching!) and it resonates louder with readers and consumers than comparable advertising.

See also: *Advertisement, Advertorial, Media Kit, Press Portfolio, Press Release, Public Relations (PR) Agent, Story.*

EDITORIAL CALENDAR: An agenda designed by publications to outline their planned editorial content for the calendar year. Publications will frequently make the calendar available to advertisers in order to attract ad revenue. However, many magazines will also publish their editorial calendar online or offer it upon request. Public relations agents and savvy entrepreneurs should request editorial calendars when building relationships with editors and interns and carefully time their press releases and pitches to coincide with the planned features of target publications.

See also: Advertising, Editorial, Public Relations (PR) Agent.

EMPLOYEE IDENTIFICATION NUMBER (EIN): A unique number issued by the federal government to identify a business entity. EIN numbers are required whenever a business operates as a corporation or partnership, or if a business has employees. They're available to businesses of all sizes and structures. Thankfully, EIN's are free of charge and can be obtained electronically in mere minutes from the Internal Revenue Service. Be prepared: some vendors request an EIN as a condition of doing business. The premise is that the presence of an EIN confirms that those requesting wholesale pricing are, in fact, a legitimate business entity. They're also known as Federal Tax Identification Numbers.

ENTREPRENEUR: My very favorite definition of an entrepreneur is provided by the Unites States Small Business Administration:

"An entrepreneur is a person who organizes and manages a business undertaking, assuming the risk for the sake of profit. An entrepreneur: Sees an opportunity. Makes a plan. Starts the business. Manages the business. Receives the profits." [2]

Can I get an *amen?*

Chances are good that if you're reading this book, you're an entrepreneur yourself. Or one in the making. Entrepreneurs are creative, courageous and tenacious. They've decided to pursue a dream and take control of their own destiny. In the year 2010, 340 of every 100,000 adults launched a business each month, resulting in 565,000 startups monthly. It's interesting to note, however, that the number of businesses being created which ultimately employee other people has been in steady decline since 2007. [3] This reflects the burgeoning number of "solopreneurs." These are entrepreneurs who work independently without taking on employees. In this challenging economic climate, those who are struggling to find a job are increasingly turning to entrepreneurship to create their own opportunities. And let's all say this together: It's important to remember that *solo* doesn't have to translate to *small*.

EXCLUSIVES:
Products or services that a business offers to a specific account. Examples might include a particular fragrance of bath bomb created especially for a big-name spa or a line of letterpress stationary created solely for a high-profile boutique. While exclusives can help get a foot in the door of much-desired account, they can also morph into black holes which suck time and resources if not carefully managed. Before you run out and buy a drum of fragrance oil and print 5,000 bath bomb labels, make certain that you've established a written agreement with regard to development costs, purchase requirements, pricing, and timelines with your client.

See also: *Incentives.*

EXCLUSIVITY AGREEMENT:
A legally binding contract between two or more entities, creating a covenant that restricts a particular business activity with other parties for a specified period of time. Generally speaking, it restricts the activities of only one of the parties' privy to the agreement. Exclusivity agreements are designed to establish predictability and stability in key strategic relationships. Examples might include the local gym positioning itself to be the singular sales outlet for Martha's Munchtastic Muffins line of Good For You Granola in the 90210 zip code. Heather's Hip Hankies might agree not to sell their unique line of handkerchiefs embroidered with the hair of angels within a 15 mile radius of Heavenly Hair Boutique.

See also: *Exclusives, Wholesale Terms.*

EXPORT PRICING:
The special price extended to overseas distributors in consideration of their purchase volumes and the additional expense of transoceanic delivery, tariffs and import taxes. Determining appropriate export prices which allow overseas distributors to turn a profit while allowing the manufacturer to also turn a profit is a delicate dance, but it can be done. The increased brand exposure and cache can offset the price reductions in spades.

See also: Commercial Invoice, Distributor, Pricing Strategy.

FEATURES:
A feature is a factual statement that describes a product or service, hopefully in a way that distinguishes it from other products or services in the marketplace.

A few examples:

- This face cream is made with argan oil.
- Our childrens' bookshelf is finished with a non-toxic paint.
- My doughnut shop is open 24 hours a day.

Features are lovely things indeed, but they are very different animals when compared to benefits. Features describe while benefits move people to buy. Knowing the difference is the cornerstone of a good marketing campaign.

For all the visual learners out there, meditate on this:

FEATURES —› ADVANTAGES —› BENEFITS = SALES

See also: Advantages, Benefits.

FOCUS GROUP:
An assembly of target consumers brought together to sample a product or service and provide measurable feedback for use in product development or marketing campaigns. Focus groups don't have to be fancy! A gathering of girlfriends over a bottle of wine can serve as a simple but valuable focus group. Make a vow to never bring a product to market without first taking it out for a test drive with a focus group, preferably several groups. They represent a critical process in the product development process.

See also: Market Research.

FREE ON BOARD (FOB):
A shipping term which indicates that the price quoted includes all charges associated with the goods until their final placement on the ultimate shipping vessel (be that a freight truck or an ocean liner). "FOB" is often followed by the city of origin (i.e. FOB San Francisco, CA). For example, let's assume you purchase 5,000 glass containers for your candle company. You can glean a few important pieces of information if the vendor's invoice indicates $7,432 FOB NY, NY:

- The product is shipping from New York City.

- As the recipient, you're responsible for all associated freight charges for the shipment after it leaves the supplier's dock in New York.

- You won't be billed separately for any palletizing fees or paperwork preparation associated with the shipment.

My company's cosmetic and spa products ship from Columbia, SC, so we often quote FOB Columbia, SC on our paperwork, but we swear that it means *"fabulousness on board."*

See also: *Pallet, Wholesale Terms.*

GOOD MANUFACTURING PRACTICES (GMP): A set of production practices that

ensure consistent, controlled product quality with each and every batch. For particular industries, GMP is federally prescribed and mandatory within the United States (i.e. medical devices and pharmaceuticals). While cosmetics, soap and personal care product manufacturers in the U.S. are not legally required to comply with federal GMP guidelines, they're still infinitely wise to implement them. Doing so ensures consistent quality from batch to batch, boosts brand credibility amongst clients and minimizes legal liabilities. GMP involves explicitly outlining standard operating procedures (SOP's), carefully training staff, keeping detailed batch records, testing raw materials and finished products, and retaining samples of finished goods, among other requirements. While GMP programs can be both confusing and overwhelming to a small business, they save time and money in the long run by reducing failed batches and streamlining processes.

I have been to Washington DC to meet with lobbyists on several occasions on behalf of trade industries representing small and micro manufacturers of personal care products in the last several years. Multiple bills have been introduced into Congress which seek to codify and mandate GMP. While none have successfully passed, there is little doubt in my mind that GMP will soon be mandatory on some level. Getting this squared away now provides a leg up on your competition, minimizes current and future liabilities, helps ensures the vitality of the company moving forward, and allows for better sleep at night.

See also: *Batch Number, Batch Record, Challenge Testing, Lot Number, Microbiology Testing, Standard Operating Procedure.*

HARMONIZED CODE: The Harmonized Commodity Description and Coding System is an internationally standardized series of six-digit numbers established by the World Customs Organization. It is used to:

- Identify and classify goods traded internationally
- Compile trade statistics
- Assign tariffs on products imported into a given country

If you want to export, you'll need to know the harmonized codes for your products. Reference appendix B for a database which can identify harmonized codes.

See also: *Commercial Invoice.*

HEAD SHOT: A type of photograph which focuses on the subject's face. Head shots are often requested by the press and having one handy will undoubtedly increase the chances of obtaining editorial coverage (three cheers for free advertising!), not to mention that professional headshots always lend a particular shine to social media efforts. It doesn't matter that you're keenly aware of the tiny crow's feet creeping in under your left eye or that your eyebrows aren't arched *just so*. Push through your self-doubt and vanity and get your head shot done. Like today. You'll thank me later... I promise.

See also: *Editorial, Media Kit.*

HERO PRODUCT: The star of your show! Hero products are those that stand out from the crowd. Hero products frequently garner media attention and shine their "halo effect" on the rest of the brand. They can be designed as heroes or become heroes organically, based on sales figures and feedback from clients. If you're designing a hero product, be certain that the product dovetails nicely with your current offerings, that it clearly and consistently embodies the company's mission and that it personifies the corporate ethos. In determining whether your company has a natural hero, look first at your sales numbers and then at customer feedback (i.e. product ratings, email communications with the company, testimonials, etc.). It's usually pretty easy to spot a hero, even if it's not sporting Bulletproof Bracelets and a Lasso of Truth. Those are *Wonder Woman®* references for those of you too young to remember my childhood hero!

IDEAL CLIENT: The customer you prefer to work with. It's who you envision buying the product. The first rule of retail is that it's impossible to please everyone. Trying to be all things to all people virtually ensures frustration and failure. The smarter approach is to carefully craft offerings based on an ideal client. To increase the chances of success, spend time getting to know your target demographic and step into their mindset. Where are they located geographically? What is their age? Income? How much education do they have? Do they have children? What do they value? What drives their purchasing decisions?

These factors may seem insignificant on the surface, but arming yourself with this knowledge empowers you to create products and services which have a built-in audience. In homage to the age old question, "Which came first: the chicken or the egg?" The ideal customer client came first. Then the product. Plotting your strategy from any other vantage point is inefficient at best and catastrophic at worst.

See also: *Branding, Focus Group, Market Research.*

WHAT WE SEE DEPENDS MAINLY ON WHAT WE LOOK FOR. ★ JOHN LUBBOCK

INCENTIVES: Rewards which are designed to illicit a specific desirable behavior.

Incentives could include:

- Offers to your wholesale clients: make an opening order of $2500 or more and receive complimentary in-store product training
- Promotions extended to retail clients: any order of $100 this week will include a FREE sampler pack of our new letterpress notecards or Orders of $50+ ship free

Smart incentives drive sales without demolishing profit margins.

See also: *Pricing Strategy, Trade Show.*

INDEPENDENT CONTRACTOR:

Congratulations! Your business is moving and shaking so well that now it's time to enlist some help. That's exciting and a bit intimidating all at the same time, eh? The first step in the hiring process should be a determination about whether the assistance you'll be obtaining will be via an independent contractor or an employee.

What's the difference? I'm so very glad you asked. The differentiation between the two generally depends on the amount of control exercised by the employer over the work being done. Independent contractors and employees are very different creatures and understanding the dissimilarity between the two is critical. Knowing the distinction between them will limit your company's liabilities and ensure that you don't raise the ire of the IRS.

INDEPENDENT CONTRACTOR	EMPLOYEE
Operates under their own business name	Operates under the banner of your business
May have their own employees	Does not have their own employees
Advertises their business services	Does not advertise their business services
Has multiple clients	Works for a singular employer
Submits invoices for work completed	Is paid hourly, salary or via commission, but does not submit invoices for payment
Sets their own hours	Has their work schedule established by someone else
Keeps business records	Does not keep business records

Many small businesses are attracted to the concept of contractors like moths to a flame. After all, independent contractors reduce their liability, afford them more flexibility in hiring and firing, and they often are accompanied by savings in labor costs. Intimidated by payroll taxes and living on shoestring budgets, many entrepreneurs jump on the independent contractor bandwagon for their first hire.

No payroll taxes! No complicated tax filings! Hip hip hooray!

Stop the train. If you have employees but cloak them as independent contractors, then the IRS can come after you in a manner which will make those employee payroll taxes look like the greatest thing that's ever happened to you.

Consequences of misclassification can include:

- Reimbursing the contractor for wages that should have been paid in a more traditional employee/employer relationship (i.e. overtime)
- Back taxes and penalties for federal and state income taxes, Social Security, Medicare and unemployment
- The payment of workers' compensation benefits that should have been in place

While there is no single litmus test for classifying independent contractors versus employees, there are some tell-tale signs.

1. **Financial:** Does the payer control how the worker is paid? Are business and travel expenses reimbursed? Is the technology (mobile phones, computers, etc.) provided by the payer to the worker? Is the worker prohibited from pursuing other business interests or collaborations?

2. **Behavioral**: Does the company dictate the work schedule? Do they control what the worker does during the day? Does the company offer training to the worker? Do they manage work flow? Do they have a voice in the selection of collaborators or others hired to work on a project? Are there systems in place to evaluate the work generated?

3. **Type of Relationship:** Are there employee-type benefits (i.e. pension plan, insurance, vacation pay, etc.)? Do you anticipate continuing the relationship after a project is complete? Is the work performed a critical aspect of the business?

Hint: If you found yourself nodding your head "yes" to multiple questions, then chances are good that you have an employee rather than a contractor. To be on the safe side, I recommend consulting an employment law attorney to verify your individual circumstances.

There are far fewer actual independent contractors in the United States than there are claimed independent contractor relationships, so tread carefully! The IRS has been cracking down on misclassified contractors in the past few years and you don't want to get caught in the crossfire.

INFRINGEMENT: A violation of an agreement or disregard for the property rights of another. Most often, creative entrepreneurs and indie business types are speaking of intellectual property rights when the word "infringement" arises.

Infringement can arrived cloaked in many forms:

- The picture of your company's felt animals shows up on a competitor's site as their own.

- The verbiage on your website, detailing the process of making those felt animals, makes its way onto a blog without your permission.

- The original design you created and screenprinted onto your company's t-shirts suddenly appears on screen-printed shirts in a local boutique, but you never sold to them.

- A new fruit-inspired body scrub is marketed in the same bottles and jars you use for your Fruitalicious Body Scrub with labels that borrow heavily from your unique design elements.

- Or perhaps the name "Fruitalicious Body Scrub" is exclusively yours because you created it and were first to market but now that pesky Frances is marketing Frances' Fruitalicious Body Scrub. The nerve!

Infringement is part and parcel of entrepreneurship and every business owner worth their salt will stare it down on one occasion or another. Don't panic: there are proven strategies for swift engagement and resolution in matters of infringement and now technology has produced a host of tools that automate IP monitoring so that you can spend your days building an empire rather than looking over your shoulder. Links to a some of my favorite technologies are included in Appendix D.

See also: *Cease & Desist, Copyright, Intellectual Property, Trade Dress, Trademark.*

INTELLECTUAL PROPERTY (IP): If your mind creates it, then it's intellectual property. There are technically two types of intellectual property:

- **Industrial:** trademarks, designs, inventions, etc.
- **Copyright:** original literary or artistic works such as novels, screenplays, marketing copy, photographs, sculpture, paintings, etc.

The beauty of IP is that it enjoys protection from the very moment of creation. Fancy government registries aren't necessary to establish ownership rights, but those registrations will be needed to pursue cases of infringement.

A critical component of entrepreneurial success hinges on the ability to develop strong, cohesive intellectual property that is original in nature and then rigorously protect that same property.

See also: *Cease & Desist, Copyright, Infringement, Trademark, Trade Dress.*

KEYSTONE PRICING (KEYSTONING): The practice of marking up goods for sale by doubling their wholesale price.

For example: You're a glassblower creating the world's most precious bud vases for flowers. After carefully considering your raw material, labor and overhead costs, you arrive at a wholesale price of $9 per vase. Gorgeous Glassworks purchases a case of your bud vases at $9 each, but they're looking to keystone your wholesale price by selling the bud vases at $18 each to end consumers.

Keystone markup is considered the gold standard in pricing, though some retailers will upcharge by 60 percent or more. When pricing products for sale, anticipate a minimum markup of 50 percent. If your products can only withstand a markup of 30-40 percent, then securing wholesale buyers will prove to be infinitely more challenging.

See also*: Manufacturer's Suggested Retail Price (MSRP), Pricing Strategy.*

KEYWORDS: Oft repeated words that explicitly identify a particular product or service. Keywords play two very important but different roles:

1. Search engines sell particular words to advertisers (that would be you!) so that businesses are more prominently featured when target customers enter those keywords into the search engine. Are you familiar with Google® AdWords? It's built upon this very premise.

2. Organic search results are those that appear thanks to their relevance, rather than compensation paid by an advertiser. Organic search engine rankings are largely derived from the keywords identified by the search engines when a site is searched and digested by their software. Correctly identifying the keywords that are most applicable to your product or service will translate into more targeted (Read here: effective and inexpensive) marketing campaigns while driving target customers to your website.

See also: *E-commerce, Search Engine Optimization (SEO).*

LABOR: The sum total of all mental and physical exertion needed to create a product. A company's pricing strategy will be heavily dependent on the cost of labor, so accurate calculations are paramount. Let's suppose your small business screen prints t-shirts with original designs created in-house. Your labor expenses would likely include the time necessary to design the shirt, generate the art, create the screen, purchase the t-shirts in bulk, unpack and inventory them, prepare the ink, apply the ink to the screen, clean your screens and workspace, process the e-commerce sale, pack the t-shirt, print a shipping label, etc.

Different types of labor will likely be assessed at different rates. For example, the artist making the design may earn $25 per hour while the helper cleaning the workspace might earn $12. Every type of pricing strategy relies heavily upon accurate labor costs, yet they can be one of the most challenging expenses for an entrepreneur to calculate.

Determining correct labor costs is dependent on four factors:

1. Including all types of the labor involved in the process of creation

2. Accurately calculating how long each of those tasks takes per item

3. Pricing the labor appropriately for each task

4. Remembering to calculate the payroll taxes required for that labor (that's how a $10 per hour job ends up costing the company $12!)

Too often, solopreneurs neglect to precisely calculate labor costs, if they calculate them at all, since they recognize themselves as the primary source of labor. If you have any ambition to scale your business, you m.u.s.t. factor labor into your equation from the very beginning. Neglecting this important exercise means that you'll either lose your ass when the time comes to hire employees, or you'll be forced to raise prices suddenly and significantly.

See also: *Cost of Goods Sold (COGS), Raw Materials, Overhead.*

LEAD TIME: The amount of time that transpires between order placement and order fulfillment. Retailers are keen on quick turnaround times, as longer turnaround times equate to empty shelves for popular items and lost revenue. If you find yourself struggling to flip orders quickly, consider instituting a few efficiencies to help speed things along and increase client retention.

See also: *Customer Service, Wholesale Terms.*

LIABILITY INSURANCE: A specific type of insurance policy protecting individuals or business entities from civil liabilities that might be incurred due to malpractice, bodily injury, property damage, or negligence. If you manufacture or distribute consumer goods, you need liability insurance. Imagine for a moment what would happen if your eye makeup remover causes an eye infection in a consumer, or your handcrafted jams and jellies develop a mold problem that makes customers sick when ingested. One valid claim can bring an otherwise stable company to its knees. If you need a referral, please locate my contact information in Appendix H of this book and be in touch. I'm happy to pass on a few names. It's of paramount importance.

See also: *Additional Insured.*

LINE SHEET: A sales tool that provides important information that wholesale buyers need to purchase your products. If catalogs and order forms were to fall in love and have a baby, line sheets would be their love child. The very best thing about line sheets? They're less expensive to generate and mail than traditional bound catalogs. Three cheers for cost savings! Line sheets should be delivered to target audiences at trade shows, on cold calls or anytime a potential buyer requests information. The most successful line sheets are visually appealing, well organized and uncluttered.

Components of a line sheet include:

- Business logo and contact information
- Wholesale terms: quick highlights of accepted payment methods, shipping options and turnaround time
- Product collection: organized by categories, such as sweaters in one section and scarves in another
- Small but stunning photos of each item
- Product details: part number, material, dimensions, price, product numbers, etc.

See also: Catalog, Wholesale Terms.

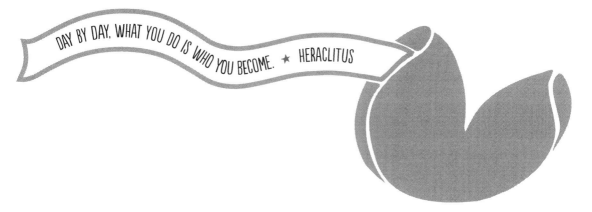

DAY BY DAY, WHAT YOU DO IS WHO YOU BECOME. ★ HERACLITUS

LOGO: The primary graphic mark of a company or brand. This is the essence of your identity and will appear on all marketing, e-commerce, communication, and brand identity material from the website to product packaging and from business card to line sheets. Logos should be scalable, meaning that the image is legible and attractive when used in large formats such as catalogs and websites and also smaller scale projects like business cards and product packaging.

The use of colors and fonts should also be carefully selected as both of these variables communicate powerful messages to audiences. Since the logo is the visual foundation of your entire brand, this is where I recommend ponying up some dough.

LOT NUMBER:
A critical component of any quality control program, lot numbers identify raw materials that are received by a company and then used in the creation of finished goods for sale. By tracking lot numbers, you ensure that the source of any material can be quickly and easily ascertained. The numbers are often issued by suppliers, but small businesses should issue lot numbers for every material and component received, even if they weren't originally provided by the vendor.

After issuing a lot number, record it in a permanent file and then apply a label indicating that lot number on the container housing the raw material. When a widget is created, whatever that lovely widget may be, the batch record will include the lot number of every component. Have a problem with a batch of finished goods? Pull the batch record, reference the lot numbers of every component and trace them back to their source.

See also: *Batch Number, Batch Record, Good Manufacturing Practice.*

MAILING LIST:
These fall into two distinct categories, traditional and email. Traditional mailing lists are compiled reports that indicate the contact details of potential customers. Those details might include the following: name, physical mailing address, age, household income, and specific marketing details (i.e. does this potential customer have children, practice a specific faith, etc.). Traditional mailing lists can be bought or rented from marketing companies or amassed organically through your company's business transactions.

The second type of list is an electronic mailing list. This list of potential customers includes email addresses, often in addition to other contact information. Electronic mailing lists are used primarily to send email communications, newsletters and promotions to customers via email. Mailing lists are worth their weight in gold and should always be managed in accordance with the company's established privacy policy.

See also: *Privacy Policy.*

MANUFACTURER'S SUGGESTED RETAIL PRICE (MSRP): The price published by manufacturers, retailers or distributors on which quantity, promotional or seasonal discounts are based. The intent is to standardize retail pricing across locations and distribution channels. It's also known as "list price."

See also: Keystone Markup, Minimum Advertised Price Policy.

MARKDOWN: The reduction of a sale price enacted to promote the movement of merchandise which isn't selling as briskly as the stockist hoped. Markdowns can swiftly erase profits for the retailer, who will be less inclined to reorder merchandise they've previously needed to mark down. For example, you manufacture ten wooden toy cars and wholesale them to Kids Need More Toys Boutique. The boutique prices each car at $10 and they sell eight of those cars during the holiday season. In January, Kids Need More Toys Boutique reduces the price of the cars from $10 to $7.50 to encourage sales. That's a markdown.

They are often expressed as percentages using this methodology:

CALCULATING MARKDOWN PERCENTAGE

Original Price − Markdown Price / Original Price x 100

$10.00 toy cars (original price) − $7.50 (markdown price)=

$2.50 divided by $10 (original price) x 100 = 25%

MARKET RESEARCH: The process of identifying potential products and markets for development. There are several genres under the general umbrella of market research.

Product research entails identifying the needs and/or desires of a specific slice of the population in order to develop products which satisfy those needs and desires.

Consumer research is the study of the motivations, preferences and behavior of a specific slice of the population in order to design marketing campaigns for maximum impact or to provide services to the ideal client in the most efficient manner.

Do not- repeat - do not launch a product or service without a thorough and concerted effort to confirm that:

- The need exists for what you're selling

- You understand precisely to whom you're marketing

Moving forward with product development without satisfying those elements is an epic waste time and resources.

See also: *Focus Group, Ideal Client, Niche.*

MEDIA KIT (PRESS KIT): A bundle of promotional materials provided to the media which tells the story behind a company or product. Though media kits have traditionally been offered in print form, digital media kits are the wave of the future.

They provide a host of benefits:

- Digital media kits can be delivered instantly via email to journalists working on a tight deadline.

- They can quickly and easily be updated as new products are introduced or the company evolves.

- They require fewer dollars to bring to fruition. Print media kits require design fees and print fees. Digital kits will likely incur design fees, but there's a small bundle to be saved without the cost of printing.

- They save trees which is a beautiful benefit in and of itself!

Ready to build a killer media kit? This handy checklist should get you started...

MEDIA KIT COMPONENT	WHAT IS IT?	DO YOU HAVE IT?
BACKGROUNDER	A concise, one page document detailing company history, key players, sales channels, timeline of growth, achievements, annual revenue, company location, etc. Essentially, the entire company distilled down to a single page.	
BIOGRAPHY	Short descriptions and photos of key players. Don't try to tell their life story; do try to add a face to the company.	
LINE SHEET	The love child of a catalog and order form. Flip back a few pages for a complete description within the very book you know hold in your hot little hands. Convenient!	
PRESS PORTFOLIO	Reprints of recent press. Keep digging…I cover press portfolios in detail a few pages over.	
PRESS RELEASE	Story pitches and new product releases.	
CONTACT INFORMATION	Often overlooked but critically important, tell members of the media who to contact within your organization to request more information or use as an interview source.	
BONUS POINTS	A disc containing videos that provide a sneak peek behind the company, headshots of key players, high-resolution product images. Be sure to add verbiage indicating that journalists may republish the images or video and be certain to include any applicable photo credits.	

See also: *Catalog, Editorial, Line Sheet, Press Portfolio, Press Release, Public Relations (PR) Agent, Story, Tear Sheet.*

MEDIA LIST: A directory of media outlets identifying key news gatherers and gatekeepers significant to a company or organization's publicity audiences. Complete media lists include the names, titles and contact information of journalists, editors or interns to whom press releases and media pitches should be directed. These are the charming people whose eyeballs you want to see the brilliant products you're offering and hear about all of the waves you're making.

Media lists are typically assembled in two ways:

1. Organically, by PR agents or individuals who are looking to build relationships centered on public relations
2. Via the assistance of either subscription services or purchased media directories

A media list is a tremendously valuable tool, but it's only worth its weight in gold if properly massaged and managed. Blindly blasting hundreds of publications with your latest press release is a vast waste of time and resources. Instead, take the time to find the publications which truly serve your target audience. Research how and what they feature.

Then either purchase a list or compile your own list of contacts within that company and direct brief, personal communications designed to serve their readers rather than promote your product or service. Contact information for several companies that maintain media lists via a subscription services can be found in Appendix G.

See also: Editorial, Press Portfolio, Press Release.

MERCHANDISING: The art and science of promoting a product at its point of sale. Merchandising not only includes the visual appeal of product packaging, but also speaks to elements in the retail environment, namely signage displayed near the products, in-store demonstrations, point-of-purchase displays, etc. Savvy manufacturers provide merchandising support either virtually or in-person to boost retail sales and provide enhanced customer service to their retailers.

See also: Packaging, Point of Purchase Display, Shelf Talker.

MERCHANT ACCOUNT: A bank account which receives the proceeds of credit card transactions. To accept credit cards, companies need to establish a bank account into which their merchant service provider can make regular deposits.

See also: *E-commerce, Merchant Service Provider, Payment Options, Secure Sockets Layer (SSL) Certificate.*

MERCHANT SERVICE PROVIDER: A company or bank that provides credit card processing for e-commerce transactions sales. Essentially, when clients discover your knock-their-socks-off website and decide to make a purchase, they enter their credit card information. That information is then processed over secure servers by a particular merchant service provider, which is designated by the company processing the sale. That merchant service provider interacts directly with Visa®, MasterCard®, American Express® et al. to complete the transaction. They collect a fee for functioning as the middle man in the service chain. If you intend to accept credit cards online, then you'll you need three things at a minimum:

- A merchant service provider
- A merchant account
- Secure Sockets Layer (SSL) Certificate

See also: *E-commerce, Merchant Account, Payment Options, Secure Sockets Layer (SSL) Certificate.*

MICROBIOLOGY TESTING: A laboratory test which detects the presence of microorganisms in a given sample to establish product safety. Microbiology tests are frequently performed on cosmetics, although food products, pharmaceuticals and water are also routinely tested. In the instance of cosmetics, while the FDA does not explicitly require microbiology testing at present, regular testing is still highly recommended as an integral part of any quality control program and as a component of good manufacturing practices. The FDA expressly prohibits the sale of products which are deemed unfit for public consumption, and lotions and potions brimming with bacteria or mold would be in violation of their mandate banning adulterated cosmetics. Though the government may not twist your arm to perform microbiology testing, taking the initiative will build credibility amongst your clients.

Trust me on this one: Nothing will crash and burn a good wholesale account faster than having clients open a jar of your fabulous face cream only to discover that it's become a petri dish of mold. Microbiology testing should yield a report detailing the APC count (total number of bacteria) as well as the presences of fungus and yeast (i.e. mold).

See also: *Batch Number, Batch Record, Challenge Testing, Good Manufacturing Practices, Quality Control Program, Standard Operating Procedures.*

SUCCESS IS HOW HIGH YOU BOUNCE AFTER YOU HIT BOTTOM. ★ GEORGE PATTON

MINIMUM ADVERTISED PRICE (MAP) POLICY:
A policy adopted by vendors mandating that particular products be advertised at or above a specific price. Though Congress has enacted laws prohibiting price fixing, MAP policies are an attempt by vendors to promote fair competition in the marketplace by restricting the advertised price for a product, though they cannot ultimately restrict the sale price of an item. As online sales blossom, more brick-and-mortar stores are becoming concerned about inherent advantages available to e-commerce merchants, namely: lower overhead costs. The result? More and more major players in the marketplace such as department stores and national grocery chains are favoring manufacturers who have instituted a MAP policy for their products.

See also: *Advertisement, Manufacturer's Suggested Retail Price (MSRP), Pricing Strategy, Wholesale Price.*

NET TERMS:
A type of trade credit which specifies that payment for goods or services is due in full x days after an order is placed. Small businesses can offer net terms to retailers and take advantage of net terms with their vendors. Net terms are traditionally followed by a number. Using "Net 30" as an example, we see that payment is due in the hands of the receiving party 30 calendar days after the order is placed.

That does not mean that on day 30, a check should be cut. No, no, no... The" 30" is the due date, not the *"let me start thinking about cutting a check"* date. Variants of the term include Net 10, Net 15, Net 60, and Net 90. Eek! Imagine waiting a full 3 months to be paid.

On occasion, a discount is offered for early payment. For example, Company X owes Business Y $10,000 for an order placed on January 1st. The $10,000 is due on or before January 31st, but Business Y may offer Company X as a 2% discount if payment is received within 15 days instead of 30. That payment formula would be expressed as 2% 15, Net 30.

Keep three caveats in mind with regard to extending net terms to your clients:

1. Ensure that your company has sufficient cash flow before offering net terms to clients.
2. Never accept credit card payments for Net 30 accounts. Not only do you have to wait for payment, but you then turn around and pay credit card processing fees on those delayed payments. Your clients should always settle their balance with a check or cash.
3. All clients who request net terms from your company should complete a credit application and your company should carefully vet that application before extending the option of net terms.

See also: *Credit Application, Payment Options, Trade Reference.*

NETWORKING:
The process of creating a group of like-minded business associates with whom you maintain communication for mutual benefit. The golden rule of networking? It should always be premised on *"How can I help?"* rather than *"What can I get?"* Traditional business networking happened almost exclusively within the local community and at industry events, but this is another brilliant example of technology having a revolutionary effect on the business world. Social networks now drive connections among business people around the world, whether or not they ever meet face-to-face. Professional networking services succeed by implementing technology to formally support networking groups which may or may not be open to the public (Read here: may or may not charge subscription fees). If there is one thing I've learned in my decade as an

entrepreneur, it's that islands are lonely and stagnant. Don't be an island. Reach out and build a tribe of compatible entrepreneurs with whom you can brainstorm, celebrate successes and offer support during challenging times.

NEWSLETTER:
A periodic update on a particular subject distributed to a specific audience. Newsletters were traditionally printed and mailed, though technology has enabled small businesses to quickly generate and disseminate attractive newsletters at minimal cost. The very best newsletters are delivered on a regular schedule: every Thursday or the first of the month or quarterly. Content could include: current promotions, press clippings, new products, recent collaborations, changes in packaging or pricing and upcoming events. My favorite newsletter software is tucked gently inside Appendix D.

See also: *Mailing List, Target Customer.*

NICHE (POINT OF DIFFERENCE):
A company's special and unique market share, created by researching the needs and desires of a particular demographic which isn't being adequately served in the current marketplace. A wise company identifies their niche and directs all of their marketing efforts in that direction to appeal to their particular ideal client. Failure to do so may mean that your soap is lost in a massive sea of soapers and your cookies are resigned to float aimlessly amidst a maze of bakers. No niche? No good.

See also: *Branding, Ideal Client, Market Research.*

NON-DISCLOSURE AGREEMENT (NDA):
A legally binding contract between two or more parties which limits how disclosed information can be used. It serves to create a confidential relationship between business parties and is often used to protect trade secrets.

Let's suppose that you've decided to outsource the production of your original handbags, because those beauties are selling faster than you can personally sew. You might request that the manufacturer taking over production sign an NDA to protect the business transaction, ensuring the manufacturer doesn't launch their own line of handbags next month that look oh-so-similar to yours. You might also want to ensure that they don't collaborate directly with your competitors. You may want an NDA as a guarantee that the manufacturer won't disassemble the purse, replicate the pattern and sell it other bag designers. In another scenario, let's assume that some hot-shot investor is batting their eyelashes at you. Either you or the investor could request an NDA before you commence the sharing financial and strategic information.   NDA's make good business sense and are wonderful for establishing parameters and outlining behavior expectations but they're notoriously challenging to enforce in a court of law. Sometimes they are called a "confidentiality agreement."

See also: *Infringement.*

ON HAND: The quantity of a particular item available for purchase via a retailer. For example, let's assume that last month you sold thirty pairs of handknit baby booties to a local boutique. At this month's sales meeting, you discover they sold twenty-two pairs of those booties. That means the store now has eight pairs of booties on hand. They need to reorder!

ONE TIME COURTESY: A customer service term which essentially means that you're willing to waive your standard policy, but just this once. I cannot for the life of me recall who first introduced me to the term, but I am eternally grateful for the introduction. I use it often in business, so often that we just call it an "OTC" around the Bella Luccè® offices. It's our polite way of letting clients know that, while we have firm policies in place, we still value their business and are willing to be flexible to retain their loyalty.

Ponder this: You're a boutique specializing in adorable vintage dresses. If your company offers a 30-day return policy on its dresses but a good client returns a dress on day thirty-two, you might offer them a one time courtesy and accept the return. In doing so, you've demonstrated your loyalty to the client while reinforcing that a clear policy is in effect. Know the term. Use the term. And I promise you'll come to love the term. It will save clients and your sanity!

See also: *Customer Service, Return Policy.*

OPEN TO BUY (OTB): A financial planning tool employed by retailers. Many small companies and specialty boutiques operate under an open to buy policy which helps guide them through purchasing decisions by allocating their available dollars for a given time period. OTB budgets are generally apportioned by month or quarter, and buyers using an OTB policy know precisely how much allowance they have left to spend on new inventory within the specified time period. Your job as a vendor is to woo the buyer to spend the highest possible percentage of their OTB budget on your merchandise.

See also: *Buyer, Stockist.*

OPENING ORDER: The first order placed with a vendor. Many companies trading in the wholesale world will offer incentives to new clients with their opening orders. Let's imagine that you operate a stylish little toy shop on Main Street. You stumble upon a new bakery making the sweetest looking cupcakes you've ever laid eyes upon and you just know they'll be an instant hit at the snack bar you offer at the toy shop. You've never before worked with this baker, but she's obviously eager to have your business. The baker might offer 10% off your opening order of cupcakes, free delivery to your store, one free cupcake for every 12 you buy at the wholesale price, or...

See also: *Incentives, Order Minimum.*

ORDER MINIMUM: A threshold established by a manufacturer as the minimum value they will accept for orders at wholesale pricing. Most, but not all, manufacturers require a minimum opening order. Subsequent reorders may have no dollar minimum at all or they may have a lower minimum than opening orders. Selling widgets one at a time at their wholesale cost gets you nowhere fast, so order minimums are established by manufactures to protect their profit margins. They may be established by dollar value (i.e. wholesale orders carry a $250 minimum) or by case-pack quantity (i.e. 12 of each item).

There are three cardinal rules which should govern the establishment of order minimums:

- You have to make a profit on every order every time. The old "onesie twosie" rarely results in profit.

- You must balance the need for robust retail displays with a buyer's desire for a minimal financial investment. Opening orders should allow for an attractive in-store display with a nice mix of your product offerings. They should not, however, require the store to max out their line of credit to get your collection through the door.

- Order minimums should be structured so that stockists can reorder as needed. Imagine that you've established a $1,000 reorder minimum. Heidi's Hipster Boutique loves your Mocha Madness Candles and they've been flying off the shelves, but your Coconut Candy Candles have stalled. That $1,000 order minimum may translate into a wait of several months as the boutique struggles to sell enough of your slow-moving inventory in order to raise enough capital and clear shelf space for the Mocha Madness they'd love to order. Chances are good that the boutique will lose interest in the interim, and that's never welcome news for you.

See also: *Opening Order, Wholesale Terms.*

OUTSOURCING: The process of contracting out a particular portion of your business. Making all those bath bombs sounded like a party until you received an order for 20,000 pieces, didn't it? You might consider outsourcing the production to a manufacturer with automated machinery to expedite lead times while keeping your costs down. Some companies outsource production. Some outsource customer service. Some outsource their public relations efforts, and some outsource nothing at all. That's the beauty of entrepreneurship: the big decisions are up to you.

See also: *Private Label.*

OVERHEAD: Any expense related to the operation of a company which isn't a fundamental part of the company's finished product or service.

Examples of overhead expenses include:

- Administrative labor (answering the phones, returning client emails, processing orders, etc.)
- Rent paid for facilities or machinery

- Utilities (phone systems, internet connection, lighting, heating, cooling)
- Insurance and legal expenses
- Advertising and marketing

Remember that overhead is one of the four pillars of **Cost Of Goods Sold (COGS)**:

RAW MATERIALS + LABOR + OVERHEAD + FREIGHT = COGS

Of those four elements, overhead expenses are usually the most challenging to accurately define for small businesses. Entrepreneurs often underestimate their overhead, which in turn brutalizes profit margins. Determining the amount of electrical energy expended in the process of creating a jar of sugar scrub or pro-rating the cost of administrative duties across a run of letterpress posters can certainly be a challenge, but it's necessary step to profitability.

See also: *Cost of Goods Sold (COGS), Labor, Pricing Strategy, Raw Materials.*

IF YOU LEARN FROM DEFEAT, YOU HAVEN'T REALLY LOST. ★ ZIG ZIGLAR

PACKAGING: Technically speaking, packaging is the sum total of the materials used to protect, handle and transport a product: bottles, jars, cigar bands, blister packs, bags, boxes, tubes, glass, plastic, cellophane, wood, paperboard, cotton... The possibilities are truly endless! Packaging is one part functionality (UPC codes, ingredient declarations for certain products, weights or dosage units, etc.) and one part marketing (branding, contact information, benefits, etc.). Well executed packaging protects the product, catches the eye, informs the consumer, drives sales, and satisfies applicable government regulations. Packaging falls under two general umbrellas, stock and custom.

	STOCK PACKAGING	CUSTOM PACKAGING
DEFINED AS	Components which are created without a specific client in mind.	Components which are made for a specific client who has agreed to purchase a minimum number.
PROPRIETARY	NO	YES
PRODUCTION	En masse, readily available	On demand
ADVANTAGES	• Low price-per-unit • No development costs • Quick delivery • No commitments • Less need to create storage space for components since packaging can be reordered at any time without lengthy lead times	• Enhanced branding • Reduced ability of competitors to replicate the style of your brand • Greater trade dress protection in cases of infringement • Ability to bring your product to market precisely as envisioned
DISADVANTAGES	• Doesn't inherently build a brand identity since any company that wishes to purchase these components may do so. • There are no restrictions that govern how, when and to whom the packaging manufacturers may sell these components.	• Developments costs • Longer lead times • Large minimum order amounts • Greater initial and ongoing investment • Need for enough space in your warehouse to house the minimum order

See also: *Branding, Merchandising, Universal Product Code.*

PALLET: A flat structure crafted of wood or rigid plastic which is used to transport goods en masse. Pallets can be loaded with boxes of widgets, drums of vegetable oil or heavy machinery, and they are typically transported via freight truck. Most pallets do not fit through standard sized doors, so manufacturers looking to work with pallets should ensure they have freight doors or double doors which can accommodate the size of a pallet. Generally speaking, loading large orders onto a pallet and shipping them via freight truck is more cost-effective than shipping loose boxes of the same weight via courier services (FedEx®, UPS®, et al.). Pallets are sometimes called "skids."

Did I ever tell you about the time I ordered my first pallet for Bella Luccè®? The shipper left the pallet at the front door of our building. We didn't have a freight door to get the pallet inside. Or a pallet jack to move the 500+ pound drums of olive and sunflower oils inside. My lack of understanding that pallets are too wide for standard doors necessitated my sleeping outside overnight next to those drums. On the sidewalk. With a sleeping bag. True story.

See also: Free on Board, Shipping Container.

PAYMENT OPTIONS: The various methods offered by a company for settling an invoice. Payment methods may include:

- Credit cards such as: Visa®, MasterCard®, American Express®, Discover®
- Transfers via bank or wire services (Western Union®)
- Cash
- Checks
- Gift certificates
- Net terms (trade credit)
- Online payment processors a la PayPal®

Practically speaking, making multiple payment options available to the customer should evolve into a greater likelihood that their interest in a product will translate into a sale of the product. However, a small business should only accept as many payment methods as they can reasonably manage. Each method carries inherent benefits and disadvantages.

Some have higher costs. Others have higher risks and still others take longer to collect.

See also: *Merchant Account, Merchant Service Provider, Net Terms, Wire Transfer.*

POINT OF PURCHASE (POP) DISPLAY:
A type of sales promotion located near the checkout which is the "point of purchase" in a retail environment. POP displays could include shelf talkers, mobiles, window decals, display stands, posters, and banners. The displays are designed to attract customer attention by focusing on products which are new, seasonal or the subject of a special promotion.

Boutiques, spas and grocery chains may inquire as to whether or not your company offers POP displays to your stockists, as these items are typically offered by the manufacturer if they're available. You may choose to provide them to accounts that order a certain volume of product within a specified period of time, to all stockists on their first order, to any stockists for a fee, or not at all. The most cost-effective varieties of POP displays are window decals, shelf talkers and posters. Sometimes these are called a "Point of Sale Display."

See also: *Branding, Merchandising, Packaging, Shelf Talker.*

PRESS PORTFOLIO:
A compilation of key press clippings from a variety of sources (newspapers, magazines, blogs, etc.) designed to highlight recent coverage of a company, product or individual. Building a press portfolio increases exposure and enhances brand credibility.

The mysterious thing about media mentions is that press begets more press. It's somewhat similar to providing your Gremlin access to water: give your single Gremlin a drink of water just once and the next time you enter the room, you'll likely have 3 Gremlins. Forgive the 80's movie reference, but I *adored* that film as a child.

Once a company has scored a few plum features, the ball seems to gain momentum and the second hit comes easier than the first. The fourth is easier than the second, and on and on.

Whenever you or your companies are the subject of a press mention, do these five things ASAP:

1. Grab a few copies at the bookstore and mail them to your mother. She's been good to you.

2. Scan digital copies of both the cover and the feature. Use your magic Photoshop® skills to merge those two images into one image that shows both the cover and your feature.

3. Add that image to the press portfolio in your digital media kit.

4. Add that image to the page of your website that shows how enamored the media is with your company. Don't have one? Make one.

5. Post that image across multiple platforms: Twitter®, Facebook®, Instagram®, Pinterest®, and your blog. Go ahead, be slightly obnoxious. You've likely worked hard to garner media attention!

6. Add the journalist's contact information to your media list and drop a handwritten "thank you" note in the mail.

See also: *Media Kit, Media List, Press Release, Tear Sheet.*

PRESS RELEASE:
A written or recorded communication directed at members of the media, announcing something newsworthy in hopes of attracting positive media attention. Press releases can be delivered via email, fax or postal mail to key news gatherers and gatekeepers at publications of interest to the company or organization releasing the communication. These might include: editors at magazines, newspaper journalists, radio stations, and television networks.

Potential triggers of a press release:

- The launch of a new product or service

- An upcoming event

- A marketing trend which dovetails nicely with a service or product on offer

- Being bestowed some type of award or honor

Press releases should be targeted to a specific audience which coincides with the audience of the publication and should contain concise information which would be of interest to their readers or viewers. These are also sometimes known as a "Media Release" or "News Release."

Appendix G at the back of this book discloses a free online tool that can instantly format your next press release for you.

See also: *Editorial, Media Kit, Press Portfolio, Public Relations (PR) Agent, Story.*

PRICING STRATEGY: The master plan for selling your widget at a price that is both attractive to consumers and profitable for your company. Pricing strategies are developed by conducting a series of exercises to precisely determine your costs including raw materials, labor, overhead, and freight, while also exploring the price of comparable products within the marketplace. To be effective, pricing strategies must account for all costs associated with bringing the product to market while also planning for all possible sales channels (i.e. retail sales, direct wholesale sales, wholesale sales through a representative who is paid commission, international distributors, etc.).

Far too many small businesses close up shop because they stay busy, but they don't generate enough profit. That represents a systemic failure in the pricing strategy: either COGS are too high or prices too low. Methodologies for determining pricing strategies are a dime a dozen, and I don't have a strong preference for one over another. However, I am of the firm opinion that to be successful, entrepreneurs must choose a particular pricing strategy and apply it consistently and precisely.

Examples of pricing strategies include:

- Bottom-up: determining COGS and multiplying by two or three to arrive at a wholesale price, four or six for arriving at a retail price
- Top down: examining the price for similar products in the marketplace, comparing your widget's quality and benefits and then pricing accordingly

See also: *Cost of Goods Sold (COGS), Distributor, Keystone Markup, Minimum Advertised Pricing Policy, Stockist, Sales Representative, and Wholesale Price.*

PRINT READY GRAPHICS: A term used in the commercial printing industry, print ready graphics are files which are in a format suitable to go directly to press. Your printer should be able to provide their individual art specifications detailing appropriate file formats and resolution, applicable bleeds, etc. If the art submitted meets these requirements, then it is considered print ready. They are also known as "Camera Ready Graphics."

See also: *Art Specifications, Dots Per Inch (DPI).*

PRIVACY POLICY: A statement informing visitors to a website about what information will be collected about their visit and how that information will be used. Every website worth its weight in salt should have a clear privacy policy linked from both the home page and every internal page of the website. The guidelines outlined therein should be attentively honored. Many merchant service providers now require a privacy policy before processing an application for their services.

PRIVATE LABEL: A product or service which is manufactured or provided by one company but marketed under a different company's brand name. Private label goods are created under contract manufacturing agreements. Common examples include: cosmetics, food, web hosting services, and customer service lines.

Private label arrangements allow companies to more quickly and easily access a market for which they see potential. They save time and allow products to be introduced to the marketplace with little or no development costs. In such instances, companies who are already manufacturing similar products but not operating at full production capacity may offer to produce under a brand name which they do not own. This has the potential to be a remarkably successful collaboration, but both companies must take care not to cannibalize each other in the marketplace by competing directly.

Let's play with two examples...

Example A: A high-profile Asian skincare company learns about a magical mushroom that, when steeped in tea, causes consumers to burn calories at twice the normal rate. A-ha! They've discovered a fantastic line extension and the ability to tap a new market segment.

The problem: the skincare company doesn't currently possess the technology or machinery to develop the mushrooms into tea. They may approach an existing small business that manufactures tea and propose a private label arrangement, allowing the skincare company to market a product under their brand name without investing in a facility, staff, machinery, or training. The tea company is happy to manufacture the tea on the skincare company's behalf, as they are now able to minimize production downtime, boosting their profitability.

Example B: Barbara's Bed & Breakfast is a quaint cottage perched on a seaside cliff. Guests have been coming to the cottage for decades and always rave on Barbara's warm hospitality and delightful cuisine. Barbara decides she wants to sell jams under the name of "Barbara's B&B" but she has absolutely zero interest in establishing a jelly factory. She discovers a private label jelly manufacturer and soon launches gourmet jams in three flavors. The brand extension is a success! Guests who come to Barbara's Bed & Breakfast are delighted to take home a souvenir that reminds them of the visit as they spread it across their toast each morning.

Bonus points: When they take their jam to the next football party, guests rave on how utterly delicious it is. Those party guests have now been introduced to Barbara's Bed & Breakfast without even stepping foot on her property.

See also: *Outsourcing.*

PRODUCT PHOTOGRAPHY: Products designed to showcase goods for sale. Pretty straightforward, right? Well, yes and no. Product photography is your single greatest weapon for communicating your brand to consumers and media influencers. You have a beautiful, user-friendly website but poorly lit photos of your sugar scrub? Consumers are likely to take a pass.

Suppose that an editor at a major fashion magazine needs companies to feature in an upcoming story about handknit legwarmers. You may create the coolest damn legwarmers on planet Earth, but if you haven't invested in professional photography, then the editor is more likely to feature Pretty Decent Legwarmer Company, despite the fact that she personally prefers your legwarmers. Pictures tell your company's story and communicate a lifestyle.

Take a long, scrutinizing look at your product photos:

- Are they selling a lifestyle?
- Are they crisp and clear?
- Are they well-lit?
- Do they communicate your brand ethos?

PRODUCTION CAPACITY:
The volume of products that can be generated by a company over a given period of time with their existing resources. Understanding your production capacity is key; knowing how to expand it is even better. So many young companies wish for success and throw themselves headlong into making it happen, only to discover that they can't keep pace when the coveted success arrives on their doorstep. The old tongue twister goes something like this: "How much wood would a woodchuck chuck if a woodchuck could chuck wood?" You probably never realized that the first person to ever utter that twister was only trying to ascertain the woodchuck's production capacity.

The real question is: *How many bath cupcakes does Susie need to make per week if QVC® places an order for 10,000 pieces and requires delivery in 8 weeks?*

PROFIT:
The difference between the amount collected (revenue) and all expenses involved in buying, operating or producing something. After tallying up all the costs of doing business, profit is what's left on the table. That profit can be used to pay dividends to shareholders- which might include you, you lucky soul!- and provide for expansion of the business in the form of new products, new machinery, new marketing campaigns, acquiring a competitor, etc.

See also: *Cost of Goods Sold (COGS), Pricing Strategy, Revenue.*

PRO FORMA INVOICE:

A pro forma invoice is a document confirming a commitment from the seller to sell goods to the buyer at the specified prices and terms. Consider pro formas as confirmed purchase orders that detail which products will be ordered at what prices. They precede the commercial invoice and are considered a binding agreement to purchase. So when you're flirting with an international distributor or a large domestic order, don't hit the "play" button until you have an agreed upon pro forma invoice. However, once you lay eyes on that beloved pro forma, consider it the starting gun of a production marathon.

See also: Commercial Invoice.

PROPRIETARY INFORMATION:

Materials or information relating to a company's products, business or activities which are privately owned and not available to the general public. Proprietary information could include, but is not limited to: financial data, trade secrets, products in development, client lists, vendor lists and formulas. Now, entrepreneurs please raise your right hand and repeat after me: "I do solemnly swear not to pose as a buyer in order to obtain my competitor's proprietary information." It's not only horrifically unprofessional and particularly brutal on the karmic scales, it's also actionable. Hint: that means illegal. Feel free to browse the websites of your competition and glean whatever information is publicly available, but never, ever cross the line of accessing private databases or marketing materials. Please and thank you.

See also: Competition, Infringement, Intellectual Property, Non-Disclosure Agreement.

PUBLIC RELATIONS (PR) AGENT:

PR agents are individuals or agencies charged with managing the flow of information between an individual, company, organization, and the public. Their primary task is to secure exposure for their clients with target audiences in arrangements that do not require direct payment (i.e. editorial). Companies invest in the services of a public relations agency to persuade the public, investors, partners and employees to maintain a certain point of view about it, its leadership and products.

PR agents who enjoy established relationships within a specific industry increase the odds of landing coverage for their client. Most agencies work on monthly retainer systems that easily total thousands of dollars per month. While outsourcing this service taps into and capitalizes upon those relationships, allowing the entrepreneur to focus on other aspects of their business, it's important to remember that PR agents have no magic wands. You can perform virtually every task in their repertoire for yourself, provided you're willing to learn their techniques and devote the time necessary to execute them consistently. A fantastic collection of public relations resources can be found in Appendix G.

See also: *Editorial.*

PURCHASE ORDER (PO):
A commercial document issued by the buyer and directed to the seller, requesting specific products or services. The purchase order generally outlines the quantities, agreed prices, payment terms and a timeline for delivery. It is an official offer of purchase and confirmation of the order by the seller makes the whole affair a legally binding contract. Technically speaking, when a customer loads up their e-commerce shopping cart and hits "submit," they are making a purchase offer. When the order is accepted by your system and a confirmation is delivered, that purchase order is confirmed and you have yourself a contract. Now, go forth and make your widgets!

See also: *Commercial Invoice, Pro Forma Invoice.*

PURCHASE MARKUP:
A formula applied by retailers to the wholesale price of goods in order to realize a profit. The purchase markup may be a flat dollar amount. For example:

> Pottery & Potions adds a flat $20 to the price of all porcelain platters purchased from Pandora's Pottery Company.

Alternately, the purchase markup may be a percentage of the price paid for the goods.

> Pottery & Potions might add 55% to the wholesale price of all porcelain platters purchased from Pandora's Pottery Company.

Whew! Just try saying that last one three times fast! In either scenario, the retailer is attracted to goods which can withstand higher purchase markups since those markups maximize profits for the retailer.

See also: *Buyer, Pricing Strategy, Stockist, Wholesale Price.*

QUALITY CONTROL PROGRAM: A series of checks and controls adopted by a company to ensure that the quality of their products or services meets established internal standards. Hold up, stop the train… What do you mean you don't have those? Quality control programs limit a company's liabilities, build credibility, increase customer retention and they should help you sleep better at night. You don't need to round up a gaggle of fancy-pants engineers, but you do need to establish internal etiquette for production processes.

Here are some ideas:

1. **Creators of gemstone earrings:** Create a checklist for incoming materials. Inspect gems for size, color variance, and clarity. Create a separate checklist for finished pieces: Are they uniform, well soldered and appropriately shaped?

2. **Bath and body manufacturers:** Create checklists for incoming materials and finished goods, standard operating procedures for all manufacturing, test water quality, etc. (*see: Good Manufacturing Practices*).

3. **Furniture makers:** Create a step-by-step checklist that is followed during manufacturing (i.e. inspect lumber for consistent grain and minimum number of knots, sand after each application of paint, use the highest-quality fasteners available, apply three coats of non-toxic paint, etc.). Have a second set of eyes check over and certify the quality of the finished piece before shipment.

4. **Consultants:** Design timelines for delivering services and rigidly adhere to them, develop customer satisfaction surveys to be delivered after your services are rendered, follow up on clients once projects are completed with a written note encouraging them to contact you with any feedback, etc.

See also: *Good Manufacturing Practices, Standard Operating Procedures.*

RAW MATERIALS: Any and all tangible components of something created. A company's pricing strategy will be heavily dependent on the cost of these materials, so accurate calculations are paramount.

Let's take a quick look at a few potential material lists for select products:

BATH BOMBS

Baking Soda	Ingredient
Citric Acid	Ingredient
Fragrance Oil	Ingredient
FD&C Colorant	Ingredient
Shrink Wrap	Packaging
Label	Packaging
Latex Gloves	Processing Aid
Hair Net	Processing Aid

WOODEN BOOK SHELF

Lumber	Ingredient
Nails	Ingredient
Fasteners	Ingredient
Non-toxic Paint	Ingredient
Sand Paper	Processing Aid
Dust Mask	Processing Aid

Processing aids are included in the material lists because they are consumed in the process of creation. Their costs should be divided amongst all items created from a batch. For example, if a pair of latex gloves costs $.50 and one pair of gloves is used to make a batch of twenty-five bath bombs, then the actual cost of the gloves per bomb is $.02 ($.50/ 25 units = $.02 per unit). Material costs are one of the four building blocks of COGS. Pro tip: Labor, overhead and freight are the others. If any material isn't included in the equation or the costs of included materials are miscalculated, then your ultimate pricing strategy will be a bust.

See also: *Pricing Strategy.*

REGISTERED MARK: That little ® you see on products or next to logos? That's a registered mark. It's the official indication that the associated trademark has been recorded as a federal registration with the United States Patent and Trademark Office (USPTO). It's now an officially protected tidbit of intellectual property. It should be noted, however, that adding that cute little "R" next to anything that has not officially been registered with the USPTO is a major no-no and can lead to charges of false advertising. Even if you have submitted a trademark application, use of the registered mark symbol is unauthorized until the mark has passed muster with the federal examining attorney, has been published for opposition and successfully passed the period of objection.

The display of the registered mark symbol is not a legal requirement for the trademark owner, though displaying it next to the trademark does contribute to an air of credibility. After all, federal trademarks don't happen overnight and they cost a bit of coin. They also tell your competitors a few things:

- That you are officially on the map
- That you know a thing or two about intellectual property
- That you plan to defend your rights to the mark

See also: *Cease & Desist, Infringement, Intellectual Property, Trade Dress, Trademark.*

LIFE SHRINKS OR EXPANDS IN PROPORTION TO ONE'S COURAGE ★ ANAIS NIN

REGULAR PRICE SELLING (RPS):
The three most appealing words that buyers and boutique owners want whispered in their ears: regular price selling. This is the process of selling a product to the end consumer at its full retail price (i.e. without discounts or promotions). RPS ensures the highest possible profit for retailers and that's precisely why the most successful businesses create goods which sell regularly at the MSRP. Products which must continually be marked down to sell are less likely to garner reorders. If you manufacture or create consumer goods, please repeat after me: "My retailer's success is my success." Why? Because when all those lovely stockists get fresh shipment of your goodness, they stock their shelves and say a prayer. And when the floodgates of consumers open, and products are snatched up quickly at maximum profit, then that buyer begins to fall madly in love with you. And buyers in love buy more. But when retailers stock their shelves and say a prayer and watch products collect dust or continually move products to higher-traffic areas with increasing markdowns to get them to move... Well, don't expect any love letters (or any reorders).

See also: *Manufacturer's Suggested Retail Price (MRSP), Markdown, Stockist.*

RETURN ON INVESTMENT (ROI): A measure of performance used to evaluate the efficiency of a program or investment. Analyzing your ROI's helps determine whether or not the company's resources are being utilized in the most efficient manner. Before undertaking a new program, product or investment, always do these four things:

- Define clear and measurable goals for the project
- Set benchmarks for progress
- Record all expenses associated with the project
- Declare a date for analysis

When that date for analysis arrives, close the loop by taking an objective look at the performance of those programs, campaigns or services and determine if the value added to your business was worth the expenditure and effort. Did you gain market share? Boost sales? Increase brand visibility? Build trust among consumers? Sometimes we're so afraid of self-analysis or so intimated by failure that we never calculate the success of our initiatives, never drill down deep enough to unearth the nuggets of wisdom that have been cultivated, even though those nuggets are powerful tools that have the potential to serve as blueprints future endeavors. Grab a pick axe and mine them regularly as they are the roadmap to your success.

RETURN POLICY: A set of protocols established by a seller outlining the conditions under which the return of their merchandise will be accepted. Return policies should be crystal clear and visible to clients at all points-of-sale, whether that's your website, your order form or your cash register.

See also: *Customer Service, Wholesale Terms.*

REVENUE: Income generated from the normal activities of a business, typically from the sale of goods or services. Revenue is traditionally measured over specific periods of time (i.e. by year or quarter). All expenses are deducted from revenue to arrive at the profit. Revenue is a beautiful thing, but profit is even prettier. Revenue means you're busy. Profit means you're making money. And making money trumps staying active any day of the week, no?

See also: *Profit.*

SALES CHANNELS:
The venues through which sales are made. There are two types of sales channels: indirect and direct. Indirect sales channels are sales by the manufacturer to an intermediary (wholesale stockists or distributors) who then resell to the end consumer. Direct sales channels are those through which a business sells directly to end consumers.

Manufacturers are wise to carefully select and control sales channels to ensure alignment with overall branding efforts. For instance, some manufactures refuse to accept individuals or businesses as a stocksist if their planned sales channel is a third party site (i.e. eBay®, Amazon®, etc.). Oftentimes, manufacturers of so-called "prestige brands" must reject offers to do business with mass retailers in order to protect the elite nature of their goods. You'd never see MAC® Cosmetics on the shelves of CVS® or Louis Vuitton® bags on the shelves at Wal-Mart®!

Domestic manufacturers looking to explore overseas markets should ensure that their contracts with international distributors explicitly define appropriate sales channels for their products, thus ensuring that your leather handbags which sell at Nordstrom® and Neiman Marcus® in the U.S. don't end up on the shelves of grocery stores in Japan. Whatever sales channels you choose, chose them wisely to ensure harmony with the brand you've worked hard to build.

See also: *Brand Dilution, Branding, Buyer, Pricing Strategy, Profit, Stockist, Sales Representative.*

SALES FORECAST:
Estimated future sales for your business. Just as you need to know next week's temperature and anticipated precipitation in order to appropriately dress your wee ones, you also need to know the climate and environment for your business within a given season. Sales forecasting involves the analysis of historical data (Read here: sales figures from previous years) and trends (Read here: industry reports of what's selling at present and the overall health of your sector) in order to manage cash flow and manage inventory. Sounds fancy, but the principal is quite simple, and it's likely you're already doing this on some level.

For instance, stationary companies build inventory for months in advance of the holiday season, knowing that November and December are peak seasons for greeting card purchases. Bath and body entrepreneurs know that they should start stockpiling holiday fragrances as soon as the weather begins to turn crisp. For years, I've known that my sales at Bella Luccè® would be lean in July and August, when so many people are on vacation and then consumed with back-to-school efforts, so I make certain we have additional cash on hand moving into lean sales months. But what do you do if you're starting a shiny new venture and you have no sales history on which to develop forecasts?

Fret not: Turn to research on your target market and competitors. This is scenario #762 in which Google® is your friend.

See also: *Cash Flow.*

SAMPLE: Items sold or given to consumers, media outlets or potential buyers which are designed to establish quality standards and allow a preview of the product before purchase. If you're launching a new perfume, you might consider slipping a sample vial inside orders for your best customers. If you've just unveiled a new variety of bread, you might slice a loaf and offer bite-sized bits to those who come into the bakery. If you think your gold and amethyst earrings are a perfect fit for a leading magazine's upcoming feature on fashion and the color purple, you'll likely send a sample pair to an editorial contact you know.

If Betty from Betty's Boutique rings your office and says that she's just discovered your company via the mystical powers of the internet and thinks they'd like to carry your lotion in her store, you might prepare a small array of samples for her, so that Betty can try all the varieties for herself, be wowed by the quality, and sign up a as a wholesale stockist.

Samples make the world of consumer goods go 'round, but you need to have a solid policy in place for distributing them. Can Suzie Q. Public (who's never placed an order with your company) send an email requesting free samples and score a few at no charge? What about Betty and her boutique? Will you send her "on the house" samples? If so, how many will she receive? Who pays for shipping? Some companies send samples at no charge and pay for the delivery; others will ship complimentary samples and only collect freight fees. Some companies offer a one-time purchase of their regular-sized product at a reduced rate. What will your sample policy be?

See also: Incentives, Wholesale Terms.

SEARCH ENGINE OPTIMIZATION (SEO):

The process of maximizing the number of visitors to a website by ensuring that its content and structure are enhanced, so that search engines can easily locate and index the site for specific keywords which speak to their target audience. Websites that diligently pursue search engine optimization rank higher in organic (i.e. unpaid) search engine results, driving traffic to their website and theoretically boosting sales. Website owners can increase search engine optimization by improving their content, ensuring that their content is unique and guaranteeing that the internal pages of their website are indexed correctly.

When selecting a web designer to build or update your website, make SEO a point of discussion but beware of cold calls from businesses offering to guarantee "placement in the top three entries of Google®!" for a specific keyword. Organic placement cannot be bought or sold and SEO waters are often shark-infested.

See also: *E-commerce.*

SECURE SOCKETS LAYER (SSL) CERTIFICATE:

An established worldwide protocol which enables parties to securely transmit information amongst them. SSL connections ensure a high level of data integrity by both encrypting the data stream and transmitting it via a secure channel. Though the technology itself is non-proprietary, a Certification Authority must issue a certificate with a key unique to the party requesting the certificate in order to establish a secure connection.

What you just read was fancy speak for this: If you plan to operate an online store which accepts credit cards, you'll need to purchase an SSL Certificate for your website. Certificates are generally renewed annually and typically cost $100-$200. Flip to Appendix D in the back of this book to discover my preferred Certification Authority.

See also: *E-commerce, Merchant Account, Merchant Service Provider, Payment Options.*

SELL SHEET: A one-page marketing tool used to describe a new product and attract the attention of the sales team, potential buyers, distributors, and/or media. Well executed sell sheets contain multiple full-color photos of the new product, a description of the product, its features and benefits, item number and/or UPC code and its specifications (dimensions, weight, etc.) Is it offered in multiple colors? Sizes? Fragrances? Media contacts go b-a-n-a-n-a-s for sell sheets because they empower editors to quickly and easily feature new products in their publications by concisely summarizing key facts. For maximum impact, print sell sheets in full color on paper with a slightly heavier weight.

See also: Catalog, Benefits, Features, Line Sheet, Product Photography, UPC Code.

SELL THROUGH PERCENTAGE: A calculation which represents how many units of an item have been sold versus how many of the same item were ordered. Example: You delivered ten of your necklaces to the Too Cute Boutique in February. In March, there were just four necklaces left in stock. Your sell through percentage is then 60%. Calculate the sell through percentage with this formula:

CALCULATING SELL THROUGH PERCENTAGES

Number of units sold / Number of units ordered x 100
6 necklaces sold / 10 necklaces ordered x 100 = 60%

SHELF LIFE: The period of time given to perishable items (food, cosmetics, etc.) before they are considered unfit for sale or consumption. Smart manufacturers are explicit about their product's shelf life, effectively communicating it to stockists and end consumers.

See also: Packaging, Quality Control Program.

SHELF TALKER: A small sign displayed alongside products in a retail setting (sometimes affixed to the actual shelf) that calls attention to a particular product by highlighting a product's features and benefits along with a call to action. Shelftalkers are a vital cog in the merchandising wheel.

See also: Branding, Call To Action, Merchandising, Point of Purchase (POP), Display.

SHIPPING CONTAINER: A standardized, reusable, resealable shipping vessel constructed of metal. Typically, shipping containers are utilized when large quantities of goods are being transported by rail car, boat or occasionally by air. Imagine how much soap or how many jars of hot sauce it would take to fill a twenty foot container (at almost twenty feet long, eight feet wide and eight feet tall)! Knowing how to securely package a shipment of this size will make or break a large order, so understanding the unique considerations of mass shipments is crucial.

See also: *Pallet, Free on Board (FOB).*

SHOWROOM: A room used to exhibit products for sale. Many sales agencies maintain permanent showrooms at large event spaces, offering a consistent display of the product lines in their repertoire, which are then incorporated into larger trade events held at that same location. In doing so, they create a perpetual venue, open to the trade, where qualified individuals can view all the lines offered by a particular agency in one space year-round. Generally speaking, sales agencies charge their manufacturers a "permanent showroom" fee which helps offset or subsidize the cost of maintaining a showroom.

See also: *Sales Representative, Trade Show.*

SOCIAL MEDIA: Interactive, internet-based platforms which allow individuals to generate and share content quickly and easily. If you own a business, you can't afford to bow out of social media. Facebook®, Twitter®, Instagram®, Pinterest®... The list goes on and on. These are the spots where consumers are gathering to share their preferences. Your website may be a thing of wonder, beautifully branded and user-friendly with a shopping cart platform that can only be described as the bee's knees. But the problem is this: people aren't there en masse.

Consider this: A recent study found that active Facebook® users spent 405 minutes per month on the website and Americans, in particular, spend more time on Facebook than any other website.[4] Meet them where they are! Create active, engaged communities on various social media platforms who are happy to support your company and evangelize your products.

Beware: Things change quickly in the world of social media. Anyone remember the all-but-abandoned MySpace®? Using a single social media platform as the principle meeting place for your brand is like building a house on quicksand. Remain diversified and willing to explore emerging technologies and platforms.

See also: *Collaboration, Networking.*

STANDARD OPERATING PROCEDURE (SOP):
A written procedure which provides the step-by-step protocol needed to perform a specific action or process that is often repeated. The aim of any SOP is to regulate that process or procedure to create a predictable, consistent outcome. If you're involved in the manufacture of any sort of consumer good, then establishing relevant SOPs is a critical task.

Their benefits are multi-fold:

1. SOPs get new staff members up and running quickly.
2. SOPs ensure all staff members are following the same protocol to yield a consistent level of quality evident in the finished goods.
3. SOPs increase credibility amongst your existing and potential clients. Look at you all fancy with the quality control program!
4. SOPs reduce overall operating expenses by minimizing failed or imperfect products.
5. SOPs limit your company's legal liabilities by minimizing the occurrence of defective products.

See also: *Good Manufacturing Practices, Quality Control Program.*

STARTUP:
An early stage in the lifecycle of a business when thoughts become actions. The idea that serves as the genesis of the enterprise begins to come to life through various activities: building the business structure, securing financing and ramping up operations. This is when I personally get on a "business high," drunk on all the excitement and forward motion. Despite all the momentum, I caution entrepreneurs to stick to their budgets, focus on their work/life balance and get plenty of sleep. Running a business is a marathon, not a sprint!

See also: *Entrepreneur, Bootstrapping.*

STOCKIST:

Think of stocksist as your potential BFFs. Stockists are retailers that stock merchandise (hopefully yours). You'll need to create a well-researched product, attractively priced and charmingly packaged in order to land on their shelves. You'll also need to offer stellar customer support, a stream of innovation and some nice buzz to stay on those shelves via reorders. The investment of time and resources necessary to secure new stockists is significantly more than what is required to retain a current stockist, so treat them well and keep in mind that their success is integral to your success. Whatever you do: never be fooled into thinking that it's the number of stockists that counts. As with almost everything in life, quality (in the form of loyal accounts who reorder frequently and are a pleasure to work with) consistently trumps quantity (number of accounts). They are sometimes known as "Retailers."

See also: Buyers.

STOCK KEEPING UNIT (SKU):

Numbers typically assigned by the manufacturer to identify each unique product for sale. Assigning SKU numbers allows for easy internal tracking of your finished goods and they simultaneously provide easier ordering for stockists purchasing your products. There are a multitude of methodologies for assigning SKU numbers, each with their own inherent advantages, but the most common misunderstanding among entrepreneurs regarding SKU's seems to center upon understanding just how many SKU's they manufacture.

- If your company creates handknit scarves in 7 colors, all from the same pattern, that equates to seven different SKU's.

- Lotion in one fragrance but in three sizes: one for the purse, one for the vanity and one for professional use in spas? Those are three separate SKU's.

Every last variant, size, color and fragrance comprises a unique product which requires a unique SKU number. When entrepreneurs take the time to individually identify their products and assign SKUs, they're often astonished at the sheer number of items they've been marketing. This is yet another instance where focus is the friend of entrepreneurs. I've been there myself as I struggle with editing my products selection. But stocking dozens of packaging components, hundreds of labels and countless raw materials makes for a complex and expensive chore. Limit your offerings by focusing on standout products and consolidate packaging whenever possible.

STORY:
The narrative that tells the "how" and "why" of your brand. Your story is the single most powerful tool in multiple entrepreneurial arsenals. In your strategic planning arsenal, your story directs decisions about what products or services you ultimately choose to offer. In your marketing arsenal, your story dictates how you approach ideal clients and win their confidence and loyalty. In your brand arsenal, your story influences the color palette and imagery you select to represent your brand.

The litmus test for a good story is composed of two factors:

- Is the story interesting? Does it leave the listener wanting to hear more?

- Are the ideas communicated by the story simple enough and clear enough for the listener to understand?

Practice telling your story. Jot it down in paper. Rehearse it in front of the mirror. Learn how to make connections, condense concepts and tell your own personal story in a way that is appealing to audiences. If you can't convey the essence of your story in sixty seconds or less, try again. Eliminate noncritical details which have value to you but fail to resonate with your audience. While stories should never be created out of thin air, they can and should be massaged to crystalize their strengths and capture attention. Your story is also known as your "Elevator Pitch."

See also: Media Kit.

SUCCESS IS THAT OLD ABC: ABILITY, BREAKS, & COURAGE ★ CHARLES LUCKMAN

SUCCESS:
It doesn't matter how I define it, it matters how *you* define it. To some, success means financial stability. The freedom to choose their future. The ability to be home every afternoon when the kids get off the school bus. The respect of peers in their industry. Knowing that they built something from scratch. Chasing a dream they've always held dear.

Working from home in their pajamas with hot tea in hand and pups at their feet... Okay, so that's my personal idea of success.

The beauty of entrepreneurship is that it allows you to define your own success, whatever form that may take. It doesn't have to mean a company that makes the Forbes® 500 list... Unless you want it to.

Try one of my favorite exercises: Grab a posterboard, a pair of scissors, a stack of magazines, and a handful of pictures of people, places and things you love. Spread the pictures out on the floor and start flipping through the magazines for images and words that personify the life you want to enjoy and the values you hold precious. Once you've amassed a nice collection, arrange and then affix them to the posterboard. Hang that posterboard somewhere prominent: in your bathroom, beside your desk or on the ceiling over your bed. That's your vision of success. Never lose sight of it. It's what will keep you centered on days when all you want is a hot bath and a week-long nap.

TEAR SHEET: A sheet "torn" from a publication as proof of publication. If your ceramic salt and pepper shakers in the shape of pomegranates (What!?!? I *have* seen them and they *do* exist.) make a splash in a major magazine, then the magazine may physically clip the feature and send a copy your way.

Not so long ago, small businesses paid big money to clipping services, who scoured the wide world of publications for mentions of their client's products, sending along a bundle of clippings each month. The company being featured might even pay a princely sum to have their clipping mounted, framed and hung on their office wall for all who entered therein to gaze up in wonder.

Hello digital age and thanks for making an appearance! Tear sheets can now be generated almost instantly and offered in virtual format, usually as a PDF. They still look darling hung on office walls, but they also appear quite dashing on websites, too. If you score a plum press mention, ask if they offer virtual tear sheets. If not, make a pilgrimage to your local bookstore to grab a few copies. Use your magical Photoshop® powers to create a tear sheet of your own by scanning the cover and the feature, then superimposing the features over a corner of the cover. Viola!

Now, assemble those tear sheets into a binder that you keep in the booth of your next trade show to dazzle would-be buyers. Display them prominently on your website to shout to the world that your company is gaining momentum. The framed versions should adorn office walls to charm visitors, and lift spirits during exhausting weeks. Also your mother should *totally* get a copy in the mail. It's the least you can do for all those grueling contractions she endured.

See also: *Editorial, Press Portfolio.*

TESTER: An item provided to a stockist either free of charge or at a reduced cost with the intention of being displayed and/or consumed in a retail environment. Suppose you make a sugar scrub and one of the product's advantages is that it rinses cleaner than other sugar scrubs in the marketplace. You might decide to offer a tester to spas offering your scrubs for sale to be placed near sinks in their restrooms, so that consumers can try the product before purchase. If you create salsa made without sugar, you might offer testers to natural food grocery stores to enable sampling while consumers cruise the aisles.

In this context, the difference between a sample and a tester is that samples are offered in packaging that offers a smaller quantity than its corresponding retail product, so that consumers can enjoy one or two bites, applications, etc. Testers are full-sized units meant to allow for sampling among multiple consumers.

Your company's wholesale terms should outline the tester policy:

- One free jar or salsa for every $250 ordered
- One free jar of salsa with every case of twenty-four
- Three free jars of salsa for opening orders only
- No free jars ever, ever but up to two half-price jars of salsa on every order

Whatever it is, determine it and proclaim it in your wholesale terms.

See also: *Incentive, Sample, Wholesale Terms.*

TESTIMONIAL: Recorded praise announcing satisfaction with a product or service. Testimonials can take many forms: emails sent to a company, reviews added to a website and videos posted on YouTube are just a few examples. Customers know that you're going to rave on your offerings; after all, you're the one that profits from the sale. But there's something about seeing Jane Q. Public proclaim the deliciousness of your doughnuts, the silky soft nature of your scarves, the comfort of your sandals, and the lightning fast delivery of her eye shadow that resonates with potential buyers and propels them into action. Collecting testimonials without being a pest is an art form.

Chew on these ideas to get you started:

1. Check to see if your e-commerce shopping cart offers a "customer review" function. Many carts now automate the collection of product reviews making them a breeze to accumulate. Offer to tuck a free sample into the customer's next order or enable them to accumulate reward points toward future discounts for all reviews left on the site.

2. Use social media to host a contest, offering a prize for the best, most outrageous, or funniest testimonial submitted within a given time period. Encourage the use of video or audio to encourage creativity and create buzz. Be certain to add verbiage which authorizes the use of those testimonials in your marketing efforts as a condition of their submission.

3. When customers dash off a particularly lovely email singing your praises, reply promptly to express your appreciation and ask their permission to use the communication as a testimonial.

See also: Customer Service.

TIME IN TRANSIT: The period of time between when a courier picks up a shipment and its delivery to the client. While you control lead times (the time it takes to process, manufacture and pack an order), the time in transit is outside your control because the products are no longer in your possession. When a client provides a definitive date by which they must have a shipment, always ensure that you accurately calculate time in transit by consulting the courier, then pad that time by a few days to account for wind, rain, snow, sleet, trucks breaking down, union strikes, etc.

See also: Lead Time, Wholesale Terms.

TIME MANAGEMENT: The process of establishing conscious control over the amount of time spent on specific activities in order to increase productivity, boost efficiency and maintain sanity. For those who have been plugging away at 9-5 careers for years, the actualization of tangible freedom afforded by entrepreneurship can be both a blessing and a curse. Hooray for working in pajamas and the ability to have a lingering lunch with a dear friend on occasion! But too often, that very freedom becomes a black hole of productivity.

You close each day by staring at a partially completed "to do" list, wondering where on the earth the day went. You habitually hit the refresh button on your email, your social media sites and your calendar in an endless cycle, paralyzed with indecision about what to do next. Sound familiar? If so, there are a range of tools, techniques and efficiencies that you can institute to set a path for each day and sprint towards the finish line. Flip to the back of this book and refer to Appendix D to discover some of my very favorite technologies designed to help implement valuable time management strategies.

TRADEMARK: A design, image, word or series of words which identify a product or service to distinguish it from the offerings of a competitor. I don't care if you make candy apples or stuffed zebras. If you're in business, it's paramount that you understand the ins and outs of basic trademark principles. A major component of your company's success is dependent upon your ability to build a brand which doesn't infringe on the work of others while simultaneously protecting your brand from the infringement of others. Myths surrounding trademarks abound. For instance, many entrepreneurs don't realize that simply using a mark in commerce instills trademark rights, even if the brand is never registered with the United States Patent and Trademark Office. However, if you plan to pursue any legal action in defense of your brand rights, then marks must be registered.

Another common myth? That two brands or products can operate under the same name, as long as they're in different classes. Not exactly. Yes, there is a *Delta* registration for bathroom faucets and another for *Delta*, as in airlines. But a registration for "Lela's Lovely" jewelry likely couldn't obtain a federal trademark registration if a trademark has already been secured for "Lela's Lovely'" eye shadow. The risk of consumer confusion as to the origin of a mark is one of the litmus tests considered by federal examining attorneys analyzing potentially competing applications.

Jewelry and eye shadow are both consumer goods marketed to women, which means one could mistakenly assume that the folks behind Lela's Lovely Earrings are the same people who bring you Lela's Lovely Eye Shadow. In that case? Application denied. Trademark law is a complicated beast, and I highly recommend the services of a qualified intellectual property attorney to help young businesses navigate the trademark maze.

See also: *Cease & Desist, Intellectual Property, Infringement, Trade Dress, Trademark.*

TRADE DRESS: A form of intellectual property, trade dress describes the

characteristics of a product's visual aesthetic and packaging that suggest the source of the product to consumers. Where trademark refers to a product name or the company that markets and/or manufacturers a product, trade dress is the sum total of various visual parts. It's the distinctive way that a product is presented which increases brand recognition in the marketplace.

Once upon a time in a land not so far away, I received an email from a concerned customer alerting me to a new company which was selling products of a nature eerily similar to Bella Luccè® in a manner eerily similar to Bella Luccè®. Now, I'm keenly aware that I didn't invent the concept of a body scrub, but my company has created innovative body scrub formulas with unique additives and aromas in packaging that is instantly recognizable as ours. This company had created similar products offered under different brand and trade names, but in packaging that would make any sane soul question whether or not it came from my company. The exact same jar, with the same lid in the same size. The same color label, with a similar product name in an identical color palette. Branding elements on those labels were arranged in a manner that was virtually indistinguishable from the layout of a typical Bella Luccè® label. Clear decals on those lids had similar medallion graphics. The. Whole. Nine. Yards.

I promptly asked my intellectual attorney to make contact. The business owner's reply? *"It's all a terrible coincidence... I've never even heard of Bella Luccè®. But no matter: the product names are different, so I'm not infringing on their trademark and I'm not changing a thing."* Gentle readers: I can only say that after a few more exchanges via my attorney, those products no longer look like ours. Lesson learned: Your widgets must not only be uniquely named and described, but they must also be uniquely presented as well.

See also: *Cease & Desist (C&D), Infringement, Intellectual Property, Trademark.*

TRADE REFERENCE: The names and contact details of businesses with which your company engages in frequent trade activity. Trade references are provided on credit applications in business-to-business transactions for the purpose of establishing a company's credit-worthiness. Exemplary trade references are worth their weight in gold and should be carefully cultivated by establishing long-term relationships with vendors and by paying invoices promptly and in full. If you decide to extend net terms to your stockists, then your company will be charged with checking the trade references submitted on credit applications. Request four or five trade references, with at least one of those coming from within your industry. Key questions to ask those references when you ring them:

- When was the account established?
- What are the payment terms (Net 30/60/90)?
- What is the current outstanding balance?
- What is the credit limit?
- What is the maximum amount owed in the account's history?
- Are payments generally prompt?

See also: *Credit Application, Net Terms.*

TRADE SHOW: An organized event open to members of a specific industry designed to showcase companies and their latest products and services. Trade shows are a collection of hundreds or thousands of related business which welcome qualified visitors over the course of several days. They can be awe-inspiring events: the sheer number of exhibitors and visitors, the cacophony that arises from the show floor, the vastness of the preparations and logistics. I once attended the largest beauty trade show in the world. Cosmoprof® Bologna is hosted in Italy each spring and boasts close to 20,000 visitors and 2,500 exhibitors in seventeen buildings... My brain literally could not process the whole of that experience.

Attending a trade show is a valuable experience, even if you're not dipping your toes in the water as an exhibitor. By attending, you gain an inside peek at market trends, have the opportunity to scope out the latest products and services from rivals and make critical industry connections. Participating in a trade show as an exhibitor can elevate brand visibility, garner media attention, present the opportunity for awards (best new product, best booth, most innovative packaging, etc.), build customer relationships with existing accounts that have representatives in attendance, and establish qualified new leads for potential customers in your target market.

Rare is there such an opportunity to kill so many birds with a single stone! But hitting a home run as a trade show exhibitor is no fluke. It requires months of preparation and research and a significant investment in resources. Small business should mediate on these questions before taking the leap:

A. **Can my company afford to participate?**

   There will be expenses a-plenty: booth fees; freight and storage fees for booth materials; union labor if you need electricity or desire help constructing the booth; travel and hotel fees for staff to attend the show; the expense of all the samples and collateral materials that will be given away; the expense of paying staff to man the booth or having extra staff work to cover shifts for those out of the office.

B. **Does this trade show speak to my target market?**

   Are the leads that will be generated qualified leads in my target market segment? Even under the banner of "spa shows," there are many subsets of tradeshows, some which have appealed to Bella Luccè® and others that have not.

   1. What is the show's niche: Natural? Organics? West Coast attendees? Resort spas or local spas? Professional treatments or retail products?

   2. Can the public attend the show as well?

   3. Do they allow cash sales from the show floor?

C. **Does my company have a strong wholesale program in place?**

   Are products designed and packaged for wholesale? Are terms and policies clearly defined? Has the process of shipping bulk orders without significant damage been refined? Does my pricing strategy allow a sufficient markup to attract buyers?

D. **What collateral materials and show incentives will compel buyers to place orders?**

   What type of samples will I make available? Will I offer a

percentage discount or free shipping for orders placed at the show? Does my company have sleek catalogs or elegant line sheets at the ready?

E. **Can I support the new business we might secure?**

Landing an onslaught of new orders without the infrastructure to support them is madness. Do you have adequate staff at present? If your business is seasonal or if this is peak season, then it's probably not the best time to dive into a trade show.

See also: *Buyer, Catalogs, Incentives, Opening Order, Sales Representatives, Samples, Sell Sheet, Showroom, Wholesale Terms.*

TRANSPARENCY: One of the greatest assets of a small business, transparency is the ability to roll back the curtain and connect with consumers by revealing information about employees, customer service, supply chains, manufacturing processes, or philanthropic efforts. Large corporations are typically faceless enterprises and they often turn green with envy when faced with Main Street America's ability to tell a story that resonates with target consumers. Small businesses sometimes feel as though Corporate America has all the advantages. After all, corporations enjoy massive resources, industry lobbyists, tax breaks, and the economy of scale working in their favor.

Well, here's your chance to shine, Small Business America! You can offer transparency in a way that few members of Corporate America can fathom. Rarely can a small business compete with a mega-corporation on price, but thankfully price isn't the sole factor with the potential to close a sale. Tell your story. Disclose your supply chain. Put your ethics on display. Showing your ideal clients the benefit that you bring to the local community and the world at large is a tremendously effective tool. Your ability to be transparent is like a golden egg, and your small business is the goose that's offering a continual supply.

Some examples:

- **Manage a bakery?** Why not post pictures taken during a tour of your local coffee roaster's facility? You sell his coffee; now tell his story and yours in the process. Emphasize that he's local. Highlight the small batch nature of his operation. Ask him for an interview and sprinkle it with humor.

- Bath and body entrepreneurs? Make a short video that highlights the handmade nature of your bath bombs. I'm not talking about whispering away your trade secrets, but show the delivery of the bags of citric acid, then Susie Q. churning that beautiful batch by hand and; finally, dozens of finished bombs drying on racks in your workshop.

- Own a novelty baby boutique? Snap pictures of your staff members, especially if they have babies! Create profiles for them on your blog with their name, hometown, how many children they have, their favorite aspect of working for your company and their favorite product sold in your shop.

TROLL: In the simpler days of childhood, trolls were mythical creatures living under the bridges of our most beloved storybooks. They usually looked quite ghastly, but were simply a literary device used to frighten. As adults and entrepreneurs, trolls have taken on a more tangible (and hairier) form altogether. Trolls are party poopers, wet blankets, maniacal critics, and cynics. They're the people who camp out in internet chat rooms, and linger on forums and slink among blog posts espousing profound ideology along the lines of:

"I don't think she's all that."

"I heard her business isn't doing as great as it appears online."

"Did you see her last product launch? I could have made that in my sleep."

"Her hair looked a hot mess in that magazine spread."

If you've been in business for any length of time, you've probably come nose-to-nose with a troll, especially if your business is making a splash. Trolls love a witty insult and they focus their energies on the object shining brightest or nearest.

There's a phenomenon among women that I have longed struggled to understand. I've dubbed it "ponytail pulling," and I loathe it with a fiery passion.

You see, women entrepreneurs are quick to whip out their pom-poms and cheer each other on. Three cheers for girlpower! Hell yes to shattering the glass ceiling! We're tremendous sources of support for one another, at least for a little while. Love and light and all of that jazz...

But then, as success for one of us flirts nearer and nearer, the pom-poms slow their pace. The jumps aren't quite as high. Women start to ponder why that one particular entrepreneur is getting all the shine. If not carefully monitored internally your "what did she do differently" can morph into "why wasn't that me?" And we all know how ugly the jealousy beast can be...

In general, we want women to succeed, but we really want *us* to succeed in particular. When we're running a marathon, happy to be in the race and feeling those endorphins, we get a little affected when we see that other woman gaining ground. As she comes into our field of vision, we spy her on our radar. Then we watch her carefully, turning around every few steps to check her progress. And then, as she begins to glide by us, we grab that chick's pony tail and pull like there's no tomorrow. *Oh no, she didn't.* Don't be a ponytail puller. Her increased pace does not ensure your imminent failure. Her win does not mitigate your finish.

The anonymity of the internet empowers trolls in a way that is fascinating to study at arm's length. The distance it allows somehow diminishes the feelings of the other person. It trivializes their pain. And the pack leader out in front throwing the nastiest barbs is often emboldened by the slobbering pack of wolves offering internet high-fives just behind her. It's a nasty affair indeed.

Listen carefully: You don't live in a storybook. Trolls may be real, but they only have the power that you surrender to them. They cannot come through your computer screen and wreck your day unless you invite them into your psyche and into your living room. Allowing them rent-free occupancy in your head reduces available space up there for creativity, inspiration and self-confidence. You're going to need lots of that, so analyze and prioritize how you delegate mental space.

If you find yourself on the receiving end of troll nastygrams, remember:

- Trolls haunt successful souls. Whether that success is personal fulfillment, media attention, financial success or enviable business networks, trolls chase things that are successful. If they are chasing you, it's because they smell success on you. Inhale deeply... I hope you smell it, too.

- Trolls thrive on attention and wither in the absence of it. Each and every time you or your posse rides in like the cavalry to slay the beasts, they multiply and fortify and grow ever stronger. You cannot outwit them. They've got the time to sit on the internet and grouse about your latest and greatest. Your time is limited because you are out there doing your latest and greatest. You will not win if you engage.

- The superpowers of trolls only exist in your head. If you refuse to give them a stage, then their sorcery evaporates. Poof! Gone! Let your mind be not bothered.

Eleanor Roosevelt once said *"No one can make you feel inferior without your permission."* Refuse them permission. They haven't earned it anyway. Know your truth, stand firm in your convictions and succeed beyond your (and their) wildest dreams. Success is the anitvenom of trolls. They'll keep clamoring for a while, you'll keep succeeding. Who wins that battle in the end?

See also: *Success.*

WHETHER YOU BELIEVE YOU CAN OR YOU BELIEVE YOU CAN'T, YOU'RE RIGHT. ★ HENRY FORD

UNIVERSAL PRODUCT CODE (UPC): A twelve-digit bar code system universally adopted throughout North America and many foreign countries which is affixed to packaging and scanned at the point-of-purchase to automate checkout and control inventory. UPC codes are doled out by GS1 US, a nonprofit group that sets standards for international commerce. If you have grand plans to gain entry into department stores or national grocers with your consumer product, then you'll need to first register for a company prefix. Each and every SKU will need its own barcode, and the fees can add up quickly.

Expect to spend $1,000 or more for a company prefix which is accompanied by a package of 100 bar codes. Some small businesses utilize UPC retailers who sell individual bar codes using their company prefix. While that's a fine and affordable solution for local stores, most mass retailers require companies to have their own UPCC company prefix, which invalidates any codes purchased through resellers.

Stop by Appendix D for valuable UPC resources.

See also: *Packaging, Stocking Keeping Units (SKU).*

VENDOR:
A person or entity offering something for sale. If you own a company producing a consumer good, then you are a vendor and you also have vendors. If you sell to XYZ Department Store, you are one of their vendors. If you buy yarn from ABC Knits, then they are one of your vendors. Simple concept, fancy business speak.

WIRE TRANSFER:
A direct transfer of funds between two parties, generally made from one bank account to another. Payments for large transactions or transactions involving foreign trade are often settled via wire transfers as they offer protection for both parties. Additionally, the fees charged by the bank are generally less expensive than credit card fees assessed by merchant account providers, especially when a significant amount of money is exchanged.

See also: *Payment Options.*

WHOLESALE PRICE:
The price of a product reserved exclusively for stockists and those reselling the product direct to consumers. The wholesale price is always lower than the retail price offered directly to the public, often by as much as fifty or even seventy percent. The discount extended to retailers is offered in consideration of bulk purchasing.

See also: *Keystone Markup, Pricing Strategy.*

WHOLESALE TERMS: The policies which govern a vendor's transaction with a retailer. Wholesale terms vary by vendor, but common components include...

- **Pricing policies**: Is there a MSRP? Are prices guided by a MAP Policy?

- **Lead times:** How long will it take for the vendor to receive the merchandise ordered?

- **Payment options:** What forms of payment are accepted?

- **Return policy:** Under what circumstances can goods be returned to the vendor and for what time period?

- **Delivery details:** How will the order be delivered to the retailer? Who pays for shipping costs? Are shipments insured?

- **Order minimums:** Does the stockist need to order a minimum dollar amount? A minimum number of units?

Having clear wholesale terms protects all parties to the transaction and establishes clear expectations.

See also: *Case Pack Quantity, Lead Time, Manufacturer's Suggested Retail Price (MSRP), Minimum Advertised Price (MAP) Policy, Order Minimum, Return Policy, Samples, Tester.*

Now, go get 'em tiger...
I'll be cheering you on as you build your empire!

Bibliography

1. Small Business Administration

http://www.sba.gov/content/what-entrepreneur

2. CNN Money®

http://money.cnn.com/2011/03/07/smallbusiness/new_business_starts/index.htm

3. U.S Census Bureau News

http://www.census.gov/retail/mrts/www/data/pdf/ec_current.pdf

4.Media Bistro®

 http://www.mediabistro.com/alltwitter/social-media-minutes_b19034

BUILD A BETTER BRAND

Branding is a complex animal, but it doesn't have to be a fang-flashing beast. Join me to discover the building blocks of a powerful brand by exploring a myriad of strategies: from color therapy to merchandising principles. We'll take a peek at several successful brands to learn what makes them tick, and decipher how their techniques can apply to your business, no matter if you're selling legwarmers or unicorn horns. The class begins with a series of exercises designed to explore your company's ethos, personality and products so that those elements can be distilled to their essence and become the core of your brand. We also chat strategies for logos, labels, packaging, collateral materials and more.

DON'T LOSE YOUR ASS

What's your pricing strategy? Do you truly understand your costs or are you stabbing in the dark? Does your pricing structure allow for direct sales to consumers, wholesaling to stores and exporting overseas without evaporating profits? If numbers make your head spin, if you're staying busy but not making money, if you're struggling to carve out a profit, then this class is right up your alley. Join me to discover methods for accurately calculating raw materials, labor and overhead. Once you know your numbers, we'll talk strategy: how to control costs, turn a profit and price goods and services for multiple sales channels and several distribution levels. Stop guessing your numbers and don't lose your ass.

ECHOING YOUR ETHOS

You've heard the lingo: *Green. Eco-friendly. Socially conscious. Fair trade.* But what does it all mean? Today's demanding consumer is flooded with choices about where to spend their dollars. Increasingly, those purchasing decisions are being made less on price and more on ethos. In this class, we'll explore various ethical marketing terms to demystify the language and understand how those attributes might apply to your venture. Together we'll dissect cause marketing campaigns, discover the ins and outs of creative corporate philanthropy and learn how to how to seamlessly weave your ethics into your brand. Practical exercises will help zero in on your passion like a heat-seeking missile and we'll finish up by exploring strategies for embodying your ethos, helping build a better world and making your company shine in a crowded marketplace.

ESTABLISHING YOUR EMPIRE

The ideas are churning, the sparks are flying, but you're not sure what to do next? Let Lucky Break be your personal guide through the entrepreneurial maze. I'd love nothing more than to help you breathe life into your idea so that you can transform that spark into a full-on solar flare. This class details various types of legal structures, the first baby steps to take as a business, how to craft a business plan, along with tips for conducting market research that propel your venture forward at warp speed. By the end, you'll have the tools and clarity you need to get your own entrepreneurial party started.

GRAB YOUR COMBAT BOOTS & LET'S GET TO BUSINESS

So you have a knock-your-socks-off idea and some thoughts on how to bring it to market, but where's the Magic Money Fairy when you need her? Bootstrapping is a strategy for starting your business without outside investment or loans. It's a practical approach that ensures you maintain 100% ownership of the company as it grows. And that level of ownership ensures control and independence: banks can't call in your loans and investors can't dictate your choices. Join me as we explore the basics of bootstrapping, discover the five core benefits of this strategy and learn practical tips for how to reinvest in your business to ensure growth while still being able to put mac-n-cheese on the table.

MAKE THEM FALL MADLY IN LOVE

Customer satisfaction is one of the most potent tools in your entrepreneurial arsenal. Your product's word on the streets needs to be über positive: filled with stories of outstanding products and happy customers who are willing to spread far and wide their affinity for you and whatever it is you do. But how do you make the masses fall hopelessly in love with your products? In this program, we'll talk "brass tacks" about customer service to define strategies and develop programs that increase customer satisfaction and boost customer retention while diffusing the grumps and mitigating their discontent. In the end, you'll walk through practical exercises to craft a "white glove" customer service strategy that inspires consumers to shout your goodness from the mountaintop. Make your company a weapon of mass satisfaction...I'll show you how.

MR. & MRS. RIGHT

Marketing to everyone will ensure you sell to almost no one. You and your products can't be all things to all people and that's precisely why identifying your ideal client is such a critical step in both product development and marketing. Let's drill down to discover your Mr. & Mrs. Right so that product offerings and marketing campaigns can be tailored for maximum efficacy among your core audience. By marrying market research with actionable wisdom, we'll crack the code of what makes your Mr. & Mrs. Right flip open their wallet and hit the "buy" button. The end result is sharper focus, leaner spending, better results and plusher profits. And seriously, who *doesn't* love that?

ROMANCING THE PRESS

If your prevailing media strategy has been to jump up and down, rabidly flailing your arms and praying that magazines and bloggers will eventually take notice, please- for the love of all things holy- have a glass of water and take a seat. Public relations isn't about throwing everything you have at the wall and seeing what sticks. It's about clarifying your story, refining your pitch, building a targeted media list, anticipating media requests and creating the tools necessary to satisfy those press inquiries at the speed of light. At the conclusion of this class, you'll know precisely what editors are looking for and how to deliver it with ease to score ridiculously fabulous press hits across a variety of digital and traditional media.

SCALING UP! *

When success comes knocking on your door, will you be ready? Beauty entrepreneurs often spend scads of time pursuing success but scant little time actually preparing for it. This innovative class teaches a variety of efficiencies for boosting current production volumes, with a special focus on personal care manufacturers. Ever wondered when to hire employees? What tasks should be hired out first? How to structure internal processes for maximum efficacy? What machines can speed things along? By exploring proven strategies developed by Bella Luccè®, we'll discover how to automate and streamline without losing the artisanal touch.

OOH LA LA...I WANNA BE IN SPAS *

Spas and salons are very different creatures than department stores, boutiques and natural health chains. If you have spas and salons in your crosshairs, then you need a unique marketing approach. Lucky for you, I've developed a winning formula for bath, body and cosmetic entrepreneurs, based on Bella Luccè®'s decade of experience in the spa industry. I've assimilated the wisdom gleaned from more than 1,000 successful spa and salon accounts to develop this innovate class designed to help you crack the spa code. We'll decrypt common treatment types and use that knowledge to build distinctive spa treatments. By the end of the class, you'll know how to price professional products, how to write treatment protocols, how to offer product education on a shoestring budget and how to deliver customer service that will have spa directors cooing.

THE RECIPE FOR WHOLESALE SUCCESS

Bella Luccè® products have successfully landed on the shelves of more than 1,000 spas and boutiques worldwide, without the benefit of a team of sales representatives. In this seminar, we'll unearth the company's top-secret techniques and discover how to apply them across industries and market segments. Learn how to establish market differentiation, streamline product offerings, craft wholesale terms, structure wholesale pricing, design persuasive collateral materials and automate ordering procedures to blow the doors off your dream accounts. Discover common pitfalls of wholesale programs and how to glide across them with ease.

THERE ARE ENOUGH HOURS IN THE DAY

Perpetually exhausted? Are those bags under your eyes semi-permanent? Is five hours of sleep your new "normal"? Entrepreneurship is not for faint of heart. It doesn't end at 5:00 each afternoon and often consumes entire weekends. Running a small business can be a particular challenge for women who might also work full-time or provide chef, chauffer, and tutoring services to their wee ones. Take heart: there are enough hours in the day to accomplish everything you need to tackle, but the keys to success lie in structure, efficiency and benchmarking. Join me to discover strategies for maximizing personal productivity to conquer more than you thought possible in a single day.

TRADE SHOW TRIUMPH

Hit it big at a trade show and you could be on the receiving end of a wave of press and a tsunami of orders. Choose the wrong show or fail to shine and you could be flushing money down the drain. Put my experience (as both exhibitor and attendee) to work for you and learn the questions you need to ask to select the right show for your business. Once you have a show in your sights, discover methods for accurately budgeting expenses, secrets for creating effective incentives and crafting compelling collateral materials. Finally, I'll reveal proven strategies for creating a big buzz on a teeny tiny budget to bring home the prize.

IMITATION ISN'T THE SINCEREST FORM OF FLATTERY

It's a story that's been repeated by entrepreneurs through time immemorial. Your web copy pops up on a competitor's website. Your unique product idea was just imitated by someone else on Etsy®. Your product photos are for sale on eBay®. Yes, it happens to all of us, but sometimes imitation really *isn't* the sincerest form of flattery. This seminar will empower you with knowledge as we define and dissect the various iterations of intellectual property. It will also arm you with a powerful array of tools designed to build a unique brand all your own and defend your brand against copycats and coat tail riders. I'll give you the blueprints for managing intellectual property without losing your mind, including technologies to automate enforcement and strategies for shutting down imposters without breaking a sweat.

YOU DOWN WITH GMP? *

Good Manufacturing Practices are a set of production guidelines prescribed by the FDA specifically for personal care manufacturers. From eye shadow to lotion and from bath fizzies to facial cleansers, all cosmetic products can benefit from adhering to GMP principles. They reduce costs, ensure the consistency of every batch, boost credibility and limit company liabilities. Because GMP was not designed with micro-manufacturers in mind, many beauty entrepreneurs stick their heads in the sand when it comes to GMP protocol. This seminar provides a bird's eye view of basic GMP codes and builds a path to compliance that doesn't require a team of engineers or a corporate-sized budget. I combine my experience as a GMP-compliant manufacturer with years of involvement in federal legislative efforts as a small business advocate to demystify GMP for even the smallest operation.

YOUR PRODUCT NEEDS A PASSPORT

Want to make a splash in Dubai? See your products in Italy? The world is your oyster, but only if you know how to pry it open. I've landed distribution deals for Bella Luccè® that span the globe, from Romania in Eastern Europe to Mauritius, a tiny island off the coast of South Africa. In fact, Bella Luccè® now sells as many products overseas as they do on U.S. soil. Tap my experience and wisdom to discover how to attract international distributors and qualify those leads without crossing the ocean. I will demystify export pricing structures and highlight critical components of distribution agreements to grow your global presence while protecting your company's bottom line.

VIRTUAL CLASSES CAN BE DOWNLOADED IN AN INSTANT AT:
www.LuckyBreakConsulting.com

Seminars accompanied by an asterisk (*) are developed especially for beauty entrepreneurs and personal care manufacturers.

APPENDIX B:

TRADE ORGANIZATIONS, BUSINESS NETWORKS & KEY GOVERNMENT AGENCIES

Food & Drug Administration (FDA)

The Food and Drug Administration (FDA) is an agency within the U.S. Department of Health and Human Services. The FDA is responsible for protecting the public health by assuring that foods are safe, wholesome, sanitary, and properly labeled; assuring cosmetics and dietary supplements are safe and properly labeled; and helping the public get the accurate science-based information they need to use medicines, devices, and foods to improve their health.
www.fda.gov

Indie Business Network

Founded in 2000 by award-winning home-based business advocate, Donna Maria Coles Johnson, Esq., IBN is a trade organization serving handmade entrepreneurs nationwide. IBN offers affordable products liability insurance, advocacy services, and coaching and mentoring services to help its members achieve their highest personal and business goals.
www.indiebusinessnetwork.com

IRS Small Business & Self Employed Tax Center

A collection of resources, printable forms and tax information for taxpayers who file Form 1040, Schedules C, E, F or Form 2106, as well as small businesses with assets under $10 million.
www.irs.gov/businesses/small/index.html

Ladies Who Launch®

Incubators, networking and live events for women entrepreneurs around the United States.
www.ladieswholaunch.com

National Association for the Self-Employed

A nonprofit, nonpartisan association providing day-to-day support, including direct access to experts, benefits, and consolidated buying power to the self-employed. Membership is open to entrepreneurs throughout the United States for an annual fee.
www.nase.org

National Association of Women Business Owners®

Representing 10 million women-owned businesses, NAWBO is the only dues-based organization representing the interests of all women entrepreneurs across all industries. It boasts over 7,000 members and 70 chapters across the country. Membership includes access to networking, legislative advocacy, an annual conference, and a host of tools and resources.
www.nawbo.org/

National Federation of Independent Businesses®

The NFIB is the leading small business association representing small and independent businesses. A nonprofit, nonpartisan organization founded in 1943, NFIB represents the consensus views of its members in Washington and all 50 state capitals. NFIB's mission is to promote and protect the right of our members to own, operate and grow their businesses. Membership provides access to research and data, networking with experts and other business owners, legal guidance, and small business advocacy at the state and federal level.
www.nfib.com/research-foundation

United States Consumer Product Safety Commission

The U.S. Consumer Product Safety Commission is charged with protecting the public from unreasonable risks of injury or death from thousands of types of consumer products under the agency's jurisdiction. Their Small Business Ombudsman provides small businesses with guidance to ensure that consumer products are in compliance with the applicable federal consumer product safety laws. They're available to assist in navigating, understanding and complying with regulations.
www.cpsc.gov

United States Department of Labor Occupational Safety & Health Administration (OSHA)

A division of the US Department of Labor, OSHA's mission is to assure safe and healthful working conditions for working men and women by setting and enforcing standards and by providing training, outreach, education, and assistance.
www.osha.gov

United States International Trade Commission

Provides an online resource for locating the harmonized codes necessary for exporting products outside the United States.
http://hts.usitc.gov/

United States Patent & Trademark Office (USPTO)

The USPTO is the federal agency that grants U.S. patents and registers. Their online database is a nice starting point for researching potential trademark conflicts when crafting company, brand or trade names. Patent and trademark applications may also be filed online.
www.uspto.gov

United States Small Business Administration (SBA)

The U.S. Small Business Administration (SBA) is an independent agency of the federal government designed to aid, counsel, assist, and protect the interests of small business concerns, to preserve free competitive enterprise and to maintain and strengthen the overall economy of our nation. They provide access to capital via business financing, entrepreneurial development via technical assistance and training, and advocacy on a federal level.
www.sba.gov

APPENDIX C: SMALL BUSINESS INFORMATION & INSPIRATION

American Express® OPEN Forum®

OPEN Forum® is an online community to exchange insights, get advice from experts, and build connections to help you power your small business success. As part of American Express® OPEN's continuing commitment to help businesses do more business, it's one of my favorite spots on the web for clear, concise tips for starting and managing a small business.
www.openforum.com

Etsy®

Billed as the "world's handmade marketplace," Etsy® is like eBay® on really fabulous, handcrafted steroids. If you can conceive it, chances are good that someone somewhere has handcrafted it and is currently selling it. It offers a phenomenal sales platform for indie and creative entrepreneurs. Grab a pot of coffee and while the day away.
www.etsy.com

Fast Company®

Billing itself as "the world's leading progressive business media brand," Fast Company® features a unique editorial focus on innovation in technology, ethical economics, leadership, and design. Written for, by, and about the most progressive business leaders, Fast Company® chronicles how changing companies create and compete, highlighting new business practices and showcasing the teams and individuals who are inventing the future and reinventing business.
www.fastcompany.com

Indie Business Blog

Hailed by Black Enterprise Magazine as "A haven for small business owners looking to grow their brand," Indie Business Blog delivers actionable sales, marketing and branding tips as well as the inspiration you and your business need to grow together to create the life of your dreams.
www.indiebusinessnetwork.com/blog

Life is Messy Bootcamp

Life is Messy Bootcamp is an online kick-in-the-pajama-pants training course for messy entrepreneurs. It's designed to give you both the flexibility to continue fueling your creative fire ("Do Not Try This At Home" experiments not sold separately) + the structure to take your brilliant ideas from light bulb to done - yawning not included. It's where neat freak meets rule breaker. Captain Obsessive Compulsive meet Dr. Chaos.
www.lifeismessybootcamp.com

Lucky Break Consulting™

Founded by Lela Barker, author of the very book you now hold in your hands, Lucky Break Consulting™ provides indispensable tools and mentoring to help emerging entrepreneurs build their empires! One-on-one consulting, personal business coaching, live workshops and digital products to refine your vision, build your brand and market it like there's no tomorrow.
www.luckybreakconsulting.com

Noisette Academy

Noisette Academy is an online training school and community that empowers creative entrepreneurs to build a business on their terms and achieve success their way. Their *Success Your Way* development program guides you through building your own strategic plan covering all areas of creative business development and then helps put it into action.
www.noisetteacademy.com

Oh My! Handmade

Oh My! Handmade is your creative community, plus best friend, biz mentor, supportive network, and enthusiastic cheerleader! Visit over 40 inspiring contributors, thousands of readers, and editor Jessika Hepburn as we explore monthly themes through daily posts and weekly #OMHG chats. From ethics to DIY branding to building a heartfelt business, and the vast galaxies in between, the OMHG community is waiting to welcome you.
www.ohmyhandmade.com

Rocket Your Revolution

This six-week online course teaches shining business ladies how to do good and do business in a BIG way...cause let's face it, It's not always about the dolla', it's changing the world that will make you holla'.
www.eringiles.com

SCORE Business Counseling

SCORE is a nonprofit organization that is federally supported to provide free business mentoring and low cost training to aspiring and existing business owners.
www.score.org

Smart Brief

Free, industry-specific newsletters delivered direct to your inbox every day. Enjoy news from any one of 25 key industries, offered in partnership with more than 100 leading trade associations.
www.smartbrief.com

Soap Queen®

A comprehensive blog with videos, photo DIY tutorials on everything from making lip balm from scratch, to soap to bath fizzies, and business advice from the trenches. Written by Washington State Small Business Person of the Year for 2011, Anne-Marie offers practical, experience-based advice on everything from how to prepare for a craft show to Business Plans 101.
www.soapqueen.com

StartupNation®

A free service founded by entrepreneurs for entrepreneurs, StartupNation bills itself as a "one-stop shop for entrepreneurial success." A tremendous resource for easy-to-follow, practical information you need to start and grow your successful business.
www.startupnation.com

Velocity Sessions by Alexandra Franzen

Alex cranks out promotional language for fiercely independent and socially-conscious entrepreneurs who want to inspire their readers, listeners, viewers, clients & customers to be more... of everything that matters. Her Velocity Sessions are full-day self-promotion & storytelling experiences to boost your business and change your life.
www.AlexandraFranzen.com

APPENDIX D: TECHNOLOGIES, EFFICIENCIES & SERVICES

Bizfilings®
The online incorporation provider of choice for more than 500,000 entrepreneurs, offering step-by-step processes that enable small business owners to incorporate or form an LLC or other business structure with ease. They also offer a full range of business filing and compliance products and tools, including Registered Agent Service in all 50 states.
www.bizfilings.com

Buy A Bar Code
Enjoy the flexibility to purchase a single UPC code at a reasonable price without the membership dues required by the Universal Code Council.
www.buyabarcode.com

Constant Contact®
Build email contact lists and generate colorful, interactive newsletters and surveys.
www.constantcontact.com

Copyscape
Your eyes and ears all over the web. For a monthly fee, register your website, and Copyscape and its bots will magically scour the web and return a weekly report indicating likely cases of infringement. It's a clever way to automate intellectual property protection.
www.copyscape.com

Dropbox
Capitalizing on cloud technology, Dropbox is a free service that lets you bring your photos, docs, and videos anywhere and share them easily. I use it frequently to manage ongoing projects and adore it for sending large files without cluttering inboxes!
www.dropbox.com

eFax
A monthly service which eliminates the need for a fax machine, Efax assigns a unique fax number that can be used locally and internationally and delivers digital faxes direct to your inbox.
www.efax.com

E-Junkie
This e-commerce solution for selling digital items online automates and secures the digital delivery of files and codes. From eBooks to mp3 tracks and software to fonts, E-Junkie offers a platform that has no transaction limit, no bandwidth limit, no setup fee and no transaction fee.
www.e-junkie.com

Evernote®
Capture screen grabs, articles, websites and notes with a click of a button and store them via cloud technology. Then access them from anywhere at any time. Enjoy their free plan or upgrade to mega-memory and enjoy file sharing for a ridiculously low monthly fee. One of my absolute favorite tools.
www.evernote.com

Expensify®
Using your phone to snap images of receipts which are then digitized and stored online for expense accounts? Pure genius.
www.expensify.com

Fotolia®
Online, royalty-free images to flesh out your website, marketing materials and more at attractive prices.
www.fotolia.com

Free Conference Call®
A free service that enables entrepreneurs to meet by phone with customers and colleagues.
www.freeconferencecall.com

Intuit® GoPayment
Enjoy the ability to accept credit cards anywhere at any time by using your phone as a processing device. Bonus points: receipts can be texted or emailed instantly to customers.
www.gopayment.com

Grasshopper®
Proclaiming that they'll make you "sound like a Fortune 500 Company," Grasshopper enables entrepreneurs to establish all variety of fancy phone structures: 800 numbers, unique extensions, call forwarding, professional voicemail recording, etc.
www.grasshopper.com

GS1®
A non-profit organization, these guys are the official gateways to UPC codes.
http://www.gs1us.org

iStock Photo®
Online, royalty-free images to flesh out your website, marketing materials and more at attractive prices.
www.istock.com

Mail Chimp®
My preferred software for building email contact lists and generating colorful, interactive newsletters and surveys.
www.mailchimp.com

Mint
Track where your pennies go quickly and free of charge. Mint compiles all of your financial accounts and information in one convenient place and uses it to create ooh-la-la visuals that enable entrepreneurs to track spending at a glance.
www.mint.com

Moo®
I adore this on-demand printing solution for small businesses. Offerings include postcards, business cards, minicards, stickers, and labels. I swoon over their colored-core Luxe business cards!
www.moo.com

PayPal®
An e-commerce platform that facilitates payments and money transfers, Paypal® can be plugged into eBay®, Etsy® and individual e-commerce websites.
www.paypal.com

PayCycle®
Payroll processing services to keep you on the straight and narrow and simplify tax filings and payments.
http://payroll.intuit.com

Price-O-Matic by Lucky Break Consulting™
If you cringe at the sight of a calculator and break out in a sweat when you see a spreadsheet, then you'll jump for joy when you see this software. Input your costs and then see the effects of various pricing strategies and multiple pricing structures for retail, wholesale and export with just a few simple clicks.
www.luckybreakconsulting.com

Survey Monkey®
Create branded, dynamic surveys for market research and customer feedback.
www.surveymonkey.com

Thawte®
Providers of Secure Sockets Layer (SSL) Certificates for e-commerce websites.
http://www.thawte.com/ssl/index.html

ToDoist
An online task manager to keep you organized, on task and efficient. ToDoist keeps you running lean and mean!
www.todoist.com

WordPress®
The greatest blogging platform in the history of Ever.
www.wordpress.com

APPENDIX E: SOCIAL MEDIA

Animoto®
Use your photos and text to create promotional videos that can be integrated across multiple social media platforms.
www.animoto.com

Bitly®
Condense and track your links- especially helpful when used in conjunction with Twitter's 140 character restriction.
www.bitly.com

Facebook®
A social networking site that now clocks more user time than any other website on the face of the planet.
www.facebook.com

Google+®
A new social media platform from your friends at Google.
www.plus.google.com

Hootsuite®
Social media management software that can harmonize multiple accounts across several social media sites.
www.hootsuite.com

Instagram®
Social media based on photo sharing. Total eye candy.
www.instagram.com

LinkedIn®
Think of it as Facebook for professionals: online resumes and business networking.
www.linkedin.com

Pinterest®
Virtual vision boards. Also known as the craftiest site on the interwebs and the greatest time suck in history. It's addictive!
www.pinterest.com

Tumblr®
A blogging platform that encourages sharing among users and is especially popular with younger demographics.
www.tumblr.com

Twitter®
Wit, wisdom, promotion and networking in a 140 characters or less, transmitted direct from your phone to the universe.
www.twitter.com

Vimeo®
A video-centric social media platform brimming with groovy artists and creative projects. The very best part? No ads.
www.vimeo.com

Wildfire®
Software designed to create, organize and promote contests across a range of social media sites.
www.wildfireapp.com

YouTube®
Videos of anything and everything uploaded by millions of people around the world. Use it to tell your story, promote contests and encourage video testimonials.
www.youtube.com

APPENDIX F: CROWDSOURCING & CROWDFUNDING

Crowdspring
Pitch your graphic design project, set a price limit, define a timeline, and let 125,000 designers compete for the honor.
www.crowdspring.com

Elance
A hot meeting spot for project owners and freelancers. Post a project and watch the bids rolls in. Choose your favorite and you're off at the races!
www.elance.com

Indiegogo®
International crowdfunding site you can tap to raise money for your next creative project or entrepreneurial adventure.
www.indiegogo.com

Kickstarter®
Very similar to Indiegogo, on a platform powered by Amazon.
www.kickstarter.com

APPENDIX G: PUBLIC RELATIONS

Bulldog Reporter
Pay-per-click for masthead information for leading journalists plus tools, tips and training for refining your pitch.
www.infocomgroup.com

Burrelles Luce
Tidbits of PR wisdom, press release distribution, editorial calendars, and more. For a fee, of course.
www.burrellesluce.com

Canada One®
A fab online tutorial for crafting effective news releases, plus a cool formatting tool to ensure it all looks polished! Bonus: It's free!
www.canadaone.com/promote/newsrelease4.html

Cision
If there is a reporter alive today on planet earth, his or her contact details appear in Cision's media database. You have to pay to play, but it is a goldmine.
http://us.cision.com/

Gift List Media
Tailored to small businesses, this condensed (but still robust) list of magazines, blogs, newspapers, and more focuses on holiday features and the press contacts that manage them.
www.giftlistmedia.com

Google® Alerts
Designate keywords in Google® (your brand name, your product names, your personal name, competitor's names, market trends, etc.) and Google® will scour the web for mentions and send daily digest updates. Think of it as a cross between your personal clipping service and a private investigator.
www.google.com/alerts

Help A Reporter Out
Journalists working on stories flash their Bat signal for sources. Lucky you, you fit the profile. Contact the journalist and land free press. Easy peasy.
www.helpareporter.com

Mastheads

Stop spending entire afternoons at the bookstore scribbling down the contact information from the mastheads of your favorite magazines! This resource collects and verifies them all so you can spend the afternoon shoe shopping instead.

www.mastheads.org

Public Relations Society of America

The leading trade industry for PR professionals in the United States. Wander over and see what wisdom you can glean.

www.prsa.org

PR Newswire®

Capitalize on their press release distribution services to get your news into hot little hands everywhere.

www.prnewswire.com

APPENDIX H: CONTACT INFORMATION FOR LELA BARKER

If you believe my consulting services would be of benefit on your entrepreneurial journey or if you'd like a complimentary referral for liability insurance coverage, please be in touch:

Lela Barker

Lucky Break Consulting, LLC
7821 St. Andrews Road #3467
Columbia, SC 29063
888.777.9436

hello@luckybreakconsulting.com

LUCKY BREAK CONSULTING

About Lela

GO BUILD YOUR EMPIRE

In 1997, Lela Barker walked away from a full university scholarship after learning that she was simultaneously pregnant and battling cancer, neither of which had been a part of her master plan. She spent the next few years trying unsuccessfully to cobble together a living and maintain her sanity. In 2002, a divorce became the catalyst that spawned her first company. With two toddlers and minimal job prospects, Lela decided to turn the skincare she'd been making as hobby into an official company. Armed with nothing but tenacity and drive, Lela transformed her initial $500 investment into a company now recognized as global industry leader.

Her Bella Luccè® spa products combine exotic ingredients from around the world into a luxurious collection that is both naturally focused and socially conscious. Bella Luccè® products are currently sold in more than 24 countries on five continents, from Los Angeles to Dubai. They've enjoyed a sell-out run on Shop at Home television and been featured in dozens of national and international publications, including: *Southern Living, Life & Style, Allure, Organic Spa, Vegetarian Times, Discover Dubai, Body + Soul, The Healing Arts Guide, Natural Health* and the *San Francisco Chronicle.*

In 2010, Lela founded a nonprofit: *From Morocco With Love™.* Inspired by a trip to Morocco to source clays and botanical oils for Bella Luccè®, she conceived a plan to import beautiful Moroccan handicrafts into the U.S. and return 100% of the profits to rural schools, with a special focus on providing educational opportunities to young girls in the indigenous Berber community. Since its inception, the organization has seeded school libraries to promote literacy, arranged critical medical care for students and provided backpacks, hygiene items, and school supplies for hundreds of young learners.

In 2012, Lela set out on another adventure: *Lucky Break Consulting*. The culmination of her decade of experience as a successful entrepreneur, *Lucky Break is* a boutique consulting firm offering a full suite of indispensable tools for those on their own entrepreneurial journey: one-on-one consulting, personal business coaching, live workshops and digital products for moguls-in-the-making.

Lela fancies herself a tried and true Southerner with a nomadic soul. She was raised in Memphis, Tennessee and is a dedicated fan of big porches and sweet tea. Over the last decade, she's visited more than twenty countries on behalf of her companies. Lela has danced in the streets of Morocco at a world music festival, crawled on her belly in the pyramids of Egypt, spent a week face down in temples on retreat in Thailand, soared above the Bedouin villages of Dubai in a hot air balloon, prayed in the Pope's home cathedral in Rome, floated in the Dead Sea of Jordan, taught business development and women's empowerment workshops in Ghana, and danced with survivors of the rebel insurgency in Uganda.

She's always delighted to find her way home to Columbia, SC to snuggle with her two spunky daughters (Chloe and Celie), patient husband (Christopher), two energetic pups (Emerson and Thoreau), two guinea pigs (Tofu and Karma) and one pretentious cat (Sasha). They keep her extraordinarily busy but unbelievably happy.

31967473R00070

Made in the USA
Charleston, SC
03 August 2014